Yahtzee Score Sheet

Name : ___________________________

Email : ___________________________

Phone : ___________________________

Other : ___________________________

Yahtzee Score Sheet

UPPER SECTION	HOW TO SCORE	GAME #1	GAME #2	GAME #3	GAME #4	GAME #5	GAME #6
Aces = 1	Count and Add Only Aces						
Twos = 2	Count and Add Only Aces						
Threes = 3	Count and Add Only Aces						
Fours = 4	Count and Add Only Aces						
Fives = 5	Count and Add Only Aces						
Sixes = 6	Count and Add Only Aces						
TOTAL SCORE	→						
BONUS If total score is 63 or over	SCORE 35						
TOTAL Of upper Section	→						

LOWER SECTION

LOWER SECTION	HOW TO SCORE	GAME #1	GAME #2	GAME #3	GAME #4	GAME #5	GAME #6
3 of a kind	Add Total Of All Dice						
4 of a kind	Add Total Of All Dice						
Full House	SCORE 25						
Sm. Straight Sequence of 4	SCORE 30						
Lg. Straight Sequence of 5	SCORE 40						
YAHTZEE of 5 a kind	SCORE 50						
Chance	Score Total Of All 5 Dice						
YAHTZEE BONUS	FOR EACH BONUS						
	SCORE 100 PER						
TOTAL Of Lower Section	→						
TOTAL Of Upper Section	→						
GRAND TOTAL	→						

Yahtzee Score Sheet

UPPER SECTION		HOW TO SCORE	GAME #1	GAME #2	GAME #3	GAME #4	GAME #5	GAME #6
Aces	= 1	Count and Add Only Aces						
Twos	= 2	Count and Add Only Aces						
Threes	= 3	Count and Add Only Aces						
Fours	= 4	Count and Add Only Aces						
Fives	= 5	Count and Add Only Aces						
Sixes	= 6	Count and Add Only Aces						
TOTAL SCORE		→						
BONUS	If total score is 63 or over	SCORE 35						
TOTAL	Of upper Section	→						

LOWER SECTION

		HOW TO SCORE	GAME #1	GAME #2	GAME #3	GAME #4	GAME #5	GAME #6
3 of a kind		Add Total Of All Dice						
4 of a kind		Add Total Of All Dice						
Full House		SCORE 25						
Sm. Straight	Sequence of 4	SCORE 30						
Lg. Straight	Sequence of 5	SCORE 40						
YAHTZEE	of 5 a kind	SCORE 50						
Chance		Score Total Of All 5 Dice						
YAHTZEE BONUS		FOR EACH BONUS						
		SCORE 100 PER						
TOTAL	Of Lower Section	→						
TOTAL	Of Upper Section	→						
GRAND TOTAL		→						

Yahtzee Score Sheet

UPPER SECTION		HOW TO SCORE	GAME #1	GAME #2	GAME #3	GAME #4	GAME #5	GAME #6
Aces	= 1	Count and Add Only Aces						
Twos	= 2	Count and Add Only Aces						
Threes	= 3	Count and Add Only Aces						
Fours	= 4	Count and Add Only Aces						
Fives	= 5	Count and Add Only Aces						
Sixes	= 6	Count and Add Only Aces						
TOTAL SCORE		→						
BONUS	If total score is 63 or over	SCORE 35						
TOTAL	Of upper Section	→						

LOWER SECTION

		HOW TO SCORE	GAME #1	GAME #2	GAME #3	GAME #4	GAME #5	GAME #6
3 of a kind		Add Total Of All Dice						
4 of a kind		Add Total Of All Dice						
Full House		SCORE 25						
Sm. Straight	Sequence of 4	SCORE 30						
Lg. Straight	Sequence of 5	SCORE 40						
YAHTZEE	of 5 a kind	SCORE 50						
Chance		Score Total Of All 5 Dice						
YAHTZEE BONUS		FOR EACH BONUS						
		SCORE 100 PER						
TOTAL	Of Lower Section	→						
TOTAL	Of Upper Section	→						
GRAND TOTAL		→						

Yahtzee Score Sheet

UPPER SECTION		HOW TO SCORE	GAME #1	GAME #2	GAME #3	GAME #4	GAME #5	GAME #6
Aces	= 1	Count and Add Only Aces						
Twos	= 2	Count and Add Only Aces						
Threes	= 3	Count and Add Only Aces						
Fours	= 4	Count and Add Only Aces						
Fives	= 5	Count and Add Only Aces						
Sixes	= 6	Count and Add Only Aces						
TOTAL SCORE		→						
BONUS	If total score is 63 or over	SCORE 35						
TOTAL	Of upper Section	→						

LOWER SECTION

			GAME #1	GAME #2	GAME #3	GAME #4	GAME #5	GAME #6
3 of a kind		Add Total Of All Dice						
4 of a kind		Add Total Of All Dice						
Full House		SCORE 25						
Sm. Straight	Sequence of 4	SCORE 30						
Lg. Straight	Sequence of 5	SCORE 40						
YAHTZEE	of 5 a kind	SCORE 50						
Chance		Score Total Of All 5 Dice						
YAHTZEE BONUS		FOR EACH BONUS						
YAHTZEE BONUS		SCORE 100 PER						
TOTAL	Of Lower Section	→						
TOTAL	Of Upper Section	→						
GRAND TOTAL		→						

Yahtzee Score Sheet

UPPER SECTION		HOW TO SCORE	GAME #1	GAME #2	GAME #3	GAME #4	GAME #5	GAME #6
Aces	= 1	Count and Add Only Aces						
Twos	= 2	Count and Add Only Aces						
Threes	= 3	Count and Add Only Aces						
Fours	= 4	Count and Add Only Aces						
Fives	= 5	Count and Add Only Aces						
Sixes	= 6	Count and Add Only Aces						
TOTAL SCORE		→						
BONUS	If total score is 63 or over	SCORE 35						
TOTAL	Of upper Section	→						

LOWER SECTION

			GAME #1	GAME #2	GAME #3	GAME #4	GAME #5	GAME #6
3 of a kind		Add Total Of All Dice						
4 of a kind		Add Total Of All Dice						
Full House		SCORE 25						
Sm. Straight	Sequence of 4	SCORE 30						
Lg. Straight	Sequence of 5	SCORE 40						
YAHTZEE	of 5 a kind	SCORE 50						
Chance		Score Total Of All 5 Dice						
YAHTZEE BONUS		FOR EACH BONUS						
		SCORE 100 PER						
TOTAL	Of Lower Section	→						
TOTAL	Of Upper Section	→						
GRAND TOTAL		→						

Yahtzee Score Sheet

UPPER SECTION	HOW TO SCORE	GAME #1	GAME #2	GAME #3	GAME #4	GAME #5	GAME #6
Aces ● = 1	Count and Add Only Aces						
Twos ● = 2	Count and Add Only Aces						
Threes ● = 3	Count and Add Only Aces						
Fours ● = 4	Count and Add Only Aces						
Fives ● = 5	Count and Add Only Aces						
Sixes ● = 6	Count and Add Only Aces						
TOTAL SCORE	→						
BONUS If total score is 63 or over	SCORE 35						
TOTAL Of upper Section	→						

LOWER SECTION

	HOW TO SCORE	GAME #1	GAME #2	GAME #3	GAME #4	GAME #5	GAME #6
3 of a kind	Add Total Of All Dice						
4 of a kind	Add Total Of All Dice						
Full House	SCORE 25						
Sm. Straight Sequence of 4	SCORE 30						
Lg. Straight Sequence of 5	SCORE 40						
YAHTZEE of 5 a kind	SCORE 50						
Chance	Score Total Of All 5 Dice						
YAHTZEE BONUS	FOR EACH BONUS						
	SCORE 100 PER						
TOTAL Of Lower Section	→						
TOTAL Of Upper Section	→						
GRAND TOTAL	→						

Yahtzee Score Sheet

UPPER SECTION		HOW TO SCORE	GAME #1	GAME #2	GAME #3	GAME #4	GAME #5	GAME #6
Aces	= 1	Count and Add Only Aces						
Twos	= 2	Count and Add Only Aces						
Threes	= 3	Count and Add Only Aces						
Fours	= 4	Count and Add Only Aces						
Fives	= 5	Count and Add Only Aces						
Sixes	= 6	Count and Add Only Aces						
TOTAL SCORE		→						
BONUS	If total score is 63 or over	SCORE 35						
TOTAL	Of upper Section	→						

LOWER SECTION

LOWER SECTION		HOW TO SCORE	GAME #1	GAME #2	GAME #3	GAME #4	GAME #5	GAME #6
3 of a kind		Add Total Of All Dice						
4 of a kind		Add Total Of All Dice						
Full House		SCORE 25						
Sm. Straight	Sequence of 4	SCORE 30						
Lg. Straight	Sequence of 5	SCORE 40						
YAHTZEE	of 5 a kind	SCORE 50						
Chance		Score Total Of All 5 Dice						
YAHTZEE BONUS		FOR EACH BONUS						
		SCORE 100 PER						
TOTAL	Of Lower Section	→						
TOTAL	Of Upper Section	→						
GRAND TOTAL		→						

Yahtzee Score Sheet

UPPER SECTION		HOW TO SCORE	GAME #1	GAME #2	GAME #3	GAME #4	GAME #5	GAME #6
Aces	= 1	Count and Add Only Aces						
Twos	= 2	Count and Add Only Aces						
Threes	= 3	Count and Add Only Aces						
Fours	= 4	Count and Add Only Aces						
Fives	= 5	Count and Add Only Aces						
Sixes	= 6	Count and Add Only Aces						
TOTAL SCORE		→						
BONUS	If total score is 63 or over	SCORE 35						
TOTAL	Of upper Section	→						

LOWER SECTION

		HOW TO SCORE	GAME #1	GAME #2	GAME #3	GAME #4	GAME #5	GAME #6
3 of a kind		Add Total Of All Dice						
4 of a kind		Add Total Of All Dice						
Full House		SCORE 25						
Sm. Straight	Sequence of 4	SCORE 30						
Lg. Straight	Sequence of 5	SCORE 40						
YAHTZEE	of 5 a kind	SCORE 50						
Chance		Score Total Of All 5 Dice						
YAHTZEE BONUS		FOR EACH BONUS						
		SCORE 100 PER						
TOTAL	Of Lower Section	→						
TOTAL	Of Upper Section	→						
GRAND TOTAL		→						

Yahtzee Score Sheet

UPPER SECTION	HOW TO SCORE	GAME #1	GAME #2	GAME #3	GAME #4	GAME #5	GAME #6
Aces • = 1	Count and Add Only Aces						
Twos = 2	Count and Add Only Aces						
Threes = 3	Count and Add Only Aces						
Fours = 4	Count and Add Only Aces						
Fives = 5	Count and Add Only Aces						
Sixes = 6	Count and Add Only Aces						
TOTAL SCORE	→						
BONUS If total score is 63 or over	SCORE 35						
TOTAL Of upper Section	→						

LOWER SECTION

	HOW TO SCORE	GAME #1	GAME #2	GAME #3	GAME #4	GAME #5	GAME #6
3 of a kind	Add Total Of All Dice						
4 of a kind	Add Total Of All Dice						
Full House	SCORE 25						
Sm. Straight Sequence of 4	SCORE 30						
Lg. Straight Sequence of 5	SCORE 40						
YAHTZEE of 5 a kind	SCORE 50						
Chance	Score Total Of All 5 Dice						
YAHTZEE BONUS	FOR EACH BONUS						
	SCORE 100 PER						
TOTAL Of Lower Section	→						
TOTAL Of Upper Section	→						
GRAND TOTAL	→						

Yahtzee Score Sheet

UPPER SECTION	HOW TO SCORE	GAME #1	GAME #2	GAME #3	GAME #4	GAME #5	GAME #6
Aces ● = 1	Count and Add Only Aces						
Twos ⠢ = 2	Count and Add Only Aces						
Threes ⠦ = 3	Count and Add Only Aces						
Fours ⠿ = 4	Count and Add Only Aces						
Fives ⚄ = 5	Count and Add Only Aces						
Sixes ⚅ = 6	Count and Add Only Aces						
TOTAL SCORE	→						
BONUS If total score is 63 or over	SCORE 35						
TOTAL Of upper Section	→						

LOWER SECTION

	HOW TO SCORE	GAME #1	GAME #2	GAME #3	GAME #4	GAME #5	GAME #6
3 of a kind	Add Total Of All Dice						
4 of a kind	Add Total Of All Dice						
Full House	SCORE 25						
Sm. Straight Sequence of 4	SCORE 30						
Lg. Straight Sequence of 5	SCORE 40						
YAHTZEE of 5 a kind	SCORE 50						
Chance	Score Total Of All 5 Dice						
YAHTZEE BONUS	FOR EACH BONUS						
	SCORE 100 PER						
TOTAL Of Lower Section	→						
TOTAL Of Upper Section	→						
GRAND TOTAL	→						

Yahtzee Score Sheet

UPPER SECTION		HOW TO SCORE	GAME #1	GAME #2	GAME #3	GAME #4	GAME #5	GAME #6
Aces	= 1	Count and Add Only Aces						
Twos	= 2	Count and Add Only Aces						
Threes	= 3	Count and Add Only Aces						
Fours	= 4	Count and Add Only Aces						
Fives	= 5	Count and Add Only Aces						
Sixes	= 6	Count and Add Only Aces						
TOTAL SCORE		→						
BONUS If total score is 63 or over		SCORE 35						
TOTAL Of upper Section		→						

LOWER SECTION

		HOW TO SCORE	GAME #1	GAME #2	GAME #3	GAME #4	GAME #5	GAME #6
3 of a kind		Add Total Of All Dice						
4 of a kind		Add Total Of All Dice						
Full House		SCORE 25						
Sm. Straight	Sequence of 4	SCORE 30						
Lg. Straight	Sequence of 5	SCORE 40						
YAHTZEE	of 5 a kind	SCORE 50						
Chance		Score Total Of All 5 Dice						
YAHTZEE BONUS		FOR EACH BONUS						
		SCORE 100 PER						
TOTAL Of Lower Section		→						
TOTAL Of Upper Section		→						
GRAND TOTAL		→						

Yahtzee Score Sheet

UPPER SECTION		HOW TO SCORE	GAME #1	GAME #2	GAME #3	GAME #4	GAME #5	GAME #6
Aces	= 1	Count and Add Only Aces						
Twos	= 2	Count and Add Only Aces						
Threes	= 3	Count and Add Only Aces						
Fours	= 4	Count and Add Only Aces						
Fives	= 5	Count and Add Only Aces						
Sixes	= 6	Count and Add Only Aces						
TOTAL SCORE		→						
BONUS	If total score is 63 or over	SCORE 35						
TOTAL	Of upper Section	→						

LOWER SECTION

		HOW TO SCORE	GAME #1	GAME #2	GAME #3	GAME #4	GAME #5	GAME #6
3 of a kind		Add Total Of All Dice						
4 of a kind		Add Total Of All Dice						
Full House		SCORE 25						
Sm. Straight	Sequence of 4	SCORE 30						
Lg. Straight	Sequence of 5	SCORE 40						
YAHTZEE	of 5 a kind	SCORE 50						
Chance		Score Total Of All 5 Dice						
YAHTZEE BONUS		FOR EACH BONUS						
		SCORE 100 PER						
TOTAL	Of Lower Section	→						
TOTAL	Of Upper Section	→						
GRAND TOTAL		→						

Yahtzee Score Sheet

UPPER SECTION	HOW TO SCORE	GAME #1	GAME #2	GAME #3	GAME #4	GAME #5	GAME #6
Aces = 1	Count and Add Only Aces						
Twos = 2	Count and Add Only Aces						
Threes = 3	Count and Add Only Aces						
Fours = 4	Count and Add Only Aces						
Fives = 5	Count and Add Only Aces						
Sixes = 6	Count and Add Only Aces						
TOTAL SCORE	→						
BONUS If total score is 63 or over	SCORE 35						
TOTAL Of upper Section	→						

LOWER SECTION

	HOW TO SCORE	GAME #1	GAME #2	GAME #3	GAME #4	GAME #5	GAME #6
3 of a kind	Add Total Of All Dice						
4 of a kind	Add Total Of All Dice						
Full House	SCORE 25						
Sm. Straight Sequence of 4	SCORE 30						
Lg. Straight Sequence of 5	SCORE 40						
YAHTZEE of 5 a kind	SCORE 50						
Chance	Score Total Of All 5 Dice						
YAHTZEE BONUS	FOR EACH BONUS						
	SCORE 100 PER						
TOTAL Of Lower Section	→						
TOTAL Of Upper Section	→						
GRAND TOTAL	→						

Yahtzee Score Sheet

UPPER SECTION		HOW TO SCORE	GAME #1	GAME #2	GAME #3	GAME #4	GAME #5	GAME #6
Aces	= 1	Count and Add Only Aces						
Twos	= 2	Count and Add Only Aces						
Threes	= 3	Count and Add Only Aces						
Fours	= 4	Count and Add Only Aces						
Fives	= 5	Count and Add Only Aces						
Sixes	= 6	Count and Add Only Aces						
TOTAL SCORE		→						
BONUS	If total score is 63 or over	SCORE 35						
TOTAL	Of upper Section	→						

LOWER SECTION

		HOW TO SCORE	GAME #1	GAME #2	GAME #3	GAME #4	GAME #5	GAME #6
3 of a kind		Add Total Of All Dice						
4 of a kind		Add Total Of All Dice						
Full House		SCORE 25						
Sm. Straight	Sequence of 4	SCORE 30						
Lg. Straight	Sequence of 5	SCORE 40						
YAHTZEE	of 5 a kind	SCORE 50						
Chance		Score Total Of All 5 Dice						
YAHTZEE BONUS		FOR EACH BONUS						
		SCORE 100 PER						
TOTAL	Of Lower Section	→						
TOTAL	Of Upper Section	→						
GRAND TOTAL		→						

Yahtzee Score Sheet

UPPER SECTION		HOW TO SCORE	GAME #1	GAME #2	GAME #3	GAME #4	GAME #5	GAME #6
Aces	• = 1	Count and Add Only Aces						
Twos	•• = 2	Count and Add Only Aces						
Threes	••• = 3	Count and Add Only Aces						
Fours	•••• = 4	Count and Add Only Aces						
Fives	••••• = 5	Count and Add Only Aces						
Sixes	•••••• = 6	Count and Add Only Aces						
TOTAL SCORE		→						
BONUS	If total score is 63 or over	SCORE 35						
TOTAL	Of upper Section	→						

LOWER SECTION

LOWER SECTION		HOW TO SCORE	GAME #1	GAME #2	GAME #3	GAME #4	GAME #5	GAME #6
3 of a kind		Add Total Of All Dice						
4 of a kind		Add Total Of All Dice						
Full House		SCORE 25						
Sm. Straight	Sequence of 4	SCORE 30						
Lg. Straight	Sequence of 5	SCORE 40						
YAHTZEE	of 5 a kind	SCORE 50						
Chance		Score Total Of All 5 Dice						
YAHTZEE BONUS		FOR EACH BONUS						
		SCORE 100 PER						
TOTAL	Of Lower Section	→						
TOTAL	Of Upper Section	→						
GRAND TOTAL		→						

Yahtzee Score Sheet

UPPER SECTION		HOW TO SCORE	GAME #1	GAME #2	GAME #3	GAME #4	GAME #5	GAME #6
Aces	= 1	Count and Add Only Aces						
Twos	= 2	Count and Add Only Aces						
Threes	= 3	Count and Add Only Aces						
Fours	= 4	Count and Add Only Aces						
Fives	= 5	Count and Add Only Aces						
Sixes	= 6	Count and Add Only Aces						
TOTAL SCORE		→						
BONUS	If total score is 63 or over	SCORE 35						
TOTAL	Of upper Section	→						

LOWER SECTION

			GAME #1	GAME #2	GAME #3	GAME #4	GAME #5	GAME #6
3 of a kind		Add Total Of All Dice						
4 of a kind		Add Total Of All Dice						
Full House		SCORE 25						
Sm. Straight	Sequence of 4	SCORE 30						
Lg. Straight	Sequence of 5	SCORE 40						
YAHTZEE	of 5 a kind	SCORE 50						
Chance		Score Total Of All 5 Dice						
YAHTZEE BONUS		FOR EACH BONUS						
		SCORE 100 PER						
TOTAL	Of Lower Section	→						
TOTAL	Of Upper Section	→						
GRAND TOTAL		→						

Yahtzee Score Sheet

UPPER SECTION		HOW TO SCORE	GAME #1	GAME #2	GAME #3	GAME #4	GAME #5	GAME #6
Aces	= 1	Count and Add Only Aces						
Twos	= 2	Count and Add Only Aces						
Threes	= 3	Count and Add Only Aces						
Fours	= 4	Count and Add Only Aces						
Fives	= 5	Count and Add Only Aces						
Sixes	= 6	Count and Add Only Aces						
TOTAL SCORE		→						
BONUS	If total score is 63 or over	SCORE 35						
TOTAL	Of upper Section	→						

LOWER SECTION

		HOW TO SCORE	GAME #1	GAME #2	GAME #3	GAME #4	GAME #5	GAME #6
3 of a kind		Add Total Of All Dice						
4 of a kind		Add Total Of All Dice						
Full House		SCORE 25						
Sm. Straight	Sequence of 4	SCORE 30						
Lg. Straight	Sequence of 5	SCORE 40						
YAHTZEE	of 5 a kind	SCORE 50						
Chance		Score Total Of All 5 Dice						
YAHTZEE BONUS		FOR EACH BONUS SCORE 100 PER						
TOTAL	Of Lower Section	→						
TOTAL	Of Upper Section	→						
GRAND TOTAL		→						

Yahtzee Score Sheet

UPPER SECTION		HOW TO SCORE	GAME #1	GAME #2	GAME #3	GAME #4	GAME #5	GAME #6
Aces	$\bullet$ = 1	Count and Add Only Aces						
Twos	= 2	Count and Add Only Aces						
Threes	= 3	Count and Add Only Aces						
Fours	= 4	Count and Add Only Aces						
Fives	= 5	Count and Add Only Aces						
Sixes	= 6	Count and Add Only Aces						
TOTAL SCORE		→						
BONUS	If total score is 63 or over	SCORE 35						
TOTAL	Of upper Section	→						

LOWER SECTION

			GAME #1	GAME #2	GAME #3	GAME #4	GAME #5	GAME #6
3 of a kind		Add Total Of All Dice						
4 of a kind		Add Total Of All Dice						
Full House		SCORE 25						
Sm. Straight	Sequence of 4	SCORE 30						
Lg. Straight	Sequence of 5	SCORE 40						
YAHTZEE	of 5 a kind	SCORE 50						
Chance		Score Total Of All 5 Dice						
YAHTZEE BONUS		FOR EACH BONUS						
		SCORE 100 PER						
TOTAL	Of Lower Section	→						
TOTAL	Of Upper Section	→						
GRAND TOTAL		→						

Yahtzee Score Sheet

UPPER SECTION		HOW TO SCORE	GAME #1	GAME #2	GAME #3	GAME #4	GAME #5	GAME #6
Aces	$\bullet$ = 1	Count and Add Only Aces						
Twos	= 2	Count and Add Only Aces						
Threes	= 3	Count and Add Only Aces						
Fours	= 4	Count and Add Only Aces						
Fives	= 5	Count and Add Only Aces						
Sixes	= 6	Count and Add Only Aces						
TOTAL SCORE		→						
BONUS	If total score is 63 or over	SCORE 35						
TOTAL	Of upper Section	→						

LOWER SECTION

		HOW TO SCORE	GAME #1	GAME #2	GAME #3	GAME #4	GAME #5	GAME #6
3 of a kind		Add Total Of All Dice						
4 of a kind		Add Total Of All Dice						
Full House		SCORE 25						
Sm. Straight	Sequence of 4	SCORE 30						
Lg. Straight	Sequence of 5	SCORE 40						
YAHTZEE	of 5 a kind	SCORE 50						
Chance		Score Total Of All 5 Dice						
YAHTZEE BONUS		FOR EACH BONUS						
		SCORE 100 PER						
TOTAL	Of Lower Section	→						
TOTAL	Of Upper Section	→						
GRAND TOTAL		→						

Yahtzee Score Sheet

UPPER SECTION			HOW TO SCORE	GAME #1	GAME #2	GAME #3	GAME #4	GAME #5	GAME #6
Aces	●	= 1	Count and Add Only Aces						
Twos		= 2	Count and Add Only Aces						
Threes		= 3	Count and Add Only Aces						
Fours		= 4	Count and Add Only Aces						
Fives		= 5	Count and Add Only Aces						
Sixes		= 6	Count and Add Only Aces						
TOTAL SCORE			→						
BONUS	If total score is 63 or over		SCORE 35						
TOTAL	Of upper Section		→						

LOWER SECTION

LOWER SECTION		HOW TO SCORE	GAME #1	GAME #2	GAME #3	GAME #4	GAME #5	GAME #6
3 of a kind		Add Total Of All Dice						
4 of a kind		Add Total Of All Dice						
Full House		SCORE 25						
Sm. Straight	Sequence of 4	SCORE 30						
Lg. Straight	Sequence of 5	SCORE 40						
YAHTZEE	of 5 a kind	SCORE 50						
Chance		Score Total Of All 5 Dice						
YAHTZEE BONUS		FOR EACH BONUS						
		SCORE 100 PER						
TOTAL	Of Lower Section	→						
TOTAL	Of Upper Section	→						
GRAND TOTAL		→						

Yahtzee Score Sheet

UPPER SECTION		HOW TO SCORE	GAME #1	GAME #2	GAME #3	GAME #4	GAME #5	GAME #6
Aces	• = 1	Count and Add Only Aces						
Twos	= 2	Count and Add Only Aces						
Threes	= 3	Count and Add Only Aces						
Fours	= 4	Count and Add Only Aces						
Fives	= 5	Count and Add Only Aces						
Sixes	= 6	Count and Add Only Aces						
TOTAL SCORE		→						
BONUS	If total score is 63 or over	SCORE 35						
TOTAL	Of upper Section	→						

LOWER SECTION

		HOW TO SCORE	GAME #1	GAME #2	GAME #3	GAME #4	GAME #5	GAME #6
3 of a kind		Add Total Of All Dice						
4 of a kind		Add Total Of All Dice						
Full House		SCORE 25						
Sm. Straight	Sequence of 4	SCORE 30						
Lg. Straight	Sequence of 5	SCORE 40						
YAHTZEE	of 5 a kind	SCORE 50						
Chance		Score Total Of All 5 Dice						
YAHTZEE BONUS		FOR EACH BONUS						
		SCORE 100 PER						
TOTAL	Of Lower Section	→						
TOTAL	Of Upper Section	→						
GRAND TOTAL		→						

Yahtzee Score Sheet

UPPER SECTION		HOW TO SCORE	GAME #1	GAME #2	GAME #3	GAME #4	GAME #5	GAME #6
Aces	= 1	Count and Add Only Aces						
Twos	= 2	Count and Add Only Aces						
Threes	= 3	Count and Add Only Aces						
Fours	= 4	Count and Add Only Aces						
Fives	= 5	Count and Add Only Aces						
Sixes	= 6	Count and Add Only Aces						
TOTAL SCORE		→						
BONUS	If total score is 63 or over	SCORE 35						
TOTAL	Of upper Section	→						

LOWER SECTION

			GAME #1	GAME #2	GAME #3	GAME #4	GAME #5	GAME #6
3 of a kind		Add Total Of All Dice						
4 of a kind		Add Total Of All Dice						
Full House		SCORE 25						
Sm. Straight	Sequence of 4	SCORE 30						
Lg. Straight	Sequence of 5	SCORE 40						
YAHTZEE	of 5 a kind	SCORE 50						
Chance		Score Total Of All 5 Dice						
YAHTZEE BONUS		FOR EACH BONUS						
		SCORE 100 PER						
TOTAL	Of Lower Section	→						
TOTAL	Of Upper Section	→						
GRAND TOTAL		→						

Yahtzee Score Sheet

UPPER SECTION		HOW TO SCORE	GAME #1	GAME #2	GAME #3	GAME #4	GAME #5	GAME #6
Aces	• = 1	Count and Add Only Aces						
Twos	= 2	Count and Add Only Aces						
Threes	= 3	Count and Add Only Aces						
Fours	= 4	Count and Add Only Aces						
Fives	= 5	Count and Add Only Aces						
Sixes	= 6	Count and Add Only Aces						
TOTAL SCORE		→						
BONUS	If total score is 63 or over	SCORE 35						
TOTAL	Of upper Section	→						

LOWER SECTION

		HOW TO SCORE	GAME #1	GAME #2	GAME #3	GAME #4	GAME #5	GAME #6
3 of a kind		Add Total Of All Dice						
4 of a kind		Add Total Of All Dice						
Full House		SCORE 25						
Sm. Straight	Sequence of 4	SCORE 30						
Lg. Straight	Sequence of 5	SCORE 40						
YAHTZEE	of 5 a kind	SCORE 50						
Chance		Score Total Of All 5 Dice						
YAHTZEE BONUS		FOR EACH BONUS						
		SCORE 100 PER						
TOTAL	Of Lower Section	→						
TOTAL	Of Upper Section	→						
GRAND TOTAL		→						

Yahtzee Score Sheet

UPPER SECTION		HOW TO SCORE	GAME #1	GAME #2	GAME #3	GAME #4	GAME #5	GAME #6
Aces	• = 1	Count and Add Only Aces						
Twos	•• = 2	Count and Add Only Aces						
Threes	••• = 3	Count and Add Only Aces						
Fours	•••• = 4	Count and Add Only Aces						
Fives	••••• = 5	Count and Add Only Aces						
Sixes	•••••• = 6	Count and Add Only Aces						
TOTAL SCORE		→						
BONUS	If total score is 63 or over	SCORE 35						
TOTAL	Of upper Section	→						

LOWER SECTION

		HOW TO SCORE	GAME #1	GAME #2	GAME #3	GAME #4	GAME #5	GAME #6
3 of a kind		Add Total Of All Dice						
4 of a kind		Add Total Of All Dice						
Full House		SCORE 25						
Sm. Straight	Sequence of 4	SCORE 30						
Lg. Straight	Sequence of 5	SCORE 40						
YAHTZEE	of 5 a kind	SCORE 50						
Chance		Score Total Of All 5 Dice						
YAHTZEE BONUS		FOR EACH BONUS						
		SCORE 100 PER						
TOTAL	Of Lower Section	→						
TOTAL	Of Upper Section	→						
GRAND TOTAL		→						

Yahtzee Score Sheet

UPPER SECTION	HOW TO SCORE	GAME #1	GAME #2	GAME #3	GAME #4	GAME #5	GAME #6
Aces • = 1	Count and Add Only Aces						
Twos = 2	Count and Add Only Aces						
Threes = 3	Count and Add Only Aces						
Fours = 4	Count and Add Only Aces						
Fives = 5	Count and Add Only Aces						
Sixes = 6	Count and Add Only Aces						
TOTAL SCORE	→						
BONUS If total score is 63 or over	SCORE 35						
TOTAL Of upper Section	→						

LOWER SECTION

	HOW TO SCORE	GAME #1	GAME #2	GAME #3	GAME #4	GAME #5	GAME #6
3 of a kind	Add Total Of All Dice						
4 of a kind	Add Total Of All Dice						
Full House	SCORE 25						
Sm. Straight Sequence of 4	SCORE 30						
Lg. Straight Sequence of 5	SCORE 40						
YAHTZEE of 5 a kind	SCORE 50						
Chance	Score Total Of All 5 Dice						
YAHTZEE BONUS	FOR EACH BONUS						
	SCORE 100 PER						
TOTAL Of Lower Section	→						
TOTAL Of Upper Section	→						
GRAND TOTAL	→						

Yahtzee Score Sheet

UPPER SECTION		HOW TO SCORE	GAME #1	GAME #2	GAME #3	GAME #4	GAME #5	GAME #6
Aces	= 1	Count and Add Only Aces						
Twos	= 2	Count and Add Only Aces						
Threes	= 3	Count and Add Only Aces						
Fours	= 4	Count and Add Only Aces						
Fives	= 5	Count and Add Only Aces						
Sixes	= 6	Count and Add Only Aces						
TOTAL SCORE		→						
BONUS	If total score is 63 or over	SCORE 35						
TOTAL	Of upper Section	→						

LOWER SECTION

LOWER SECTION		HOW TO SCORE	GAME #1	GAME #2	GAME #3	GAME #4	GAME #5	GAME #6
3 of a kind		Add Total Of All Dice						
4 of a kind		Add Total Of All Dice						
Full House		SCORE 25						
Sm. Straight	Sequence of 4	SCORE 30						
Lg. Straight	Sequence of 5	SCORE 40						
YAHTZEE	of 5 a kind	SCORE 50						
Chance		Score Total Of All 5 Dice						
YAHTZEE BONUS		FOR EACH BONUS						
		SCORE 100 PER						
TOTAL	Of Lower Section	→						
TOTAL	Of Upper Section	→						
GRAND TOTAL		→						

Yahtzee Score Sheet

UPPER SECTION	HOW TO SCORE	GAME #1	GAME #2	GAME #3	GAME #4	GAME #5	GAME #6
Aces • = 1	Count and Add Only Aces						
Twos = 2	Count and Add Only Aces						
Threes = 3	Count and Add Only Aces						
Fours = 4	Count and Add Only Aces						
Fives = 5	Count and Add Only Aces						
Sixes = 6	Count and Add Only Aces						
TOTAL SCORE	→						
BONUS If total score is 63 or over	SCORE 35						
TOTAL Of upper Section	→						

LOWER SECTION

	HOW TO SCORE	GAME #1	GAME #2	GAME #3	GAME #4	GAME #5	GAME #6
3 of a kind	Add Total Of All Dice						
4 of a kind	Add Total Of All Dice						
Full House	SCORE 25						
Sm. Straight Sequence of 4	SCORE 30						
Lg. Straight Sequence of 5	SCORE 40						
YAHTZEE of 5 a kind	SCORE 50						
Chance	Score Total Of All 5 Dice						
YAHTZEE BONUS	FOR EACH BONUS						
	SCORE 100 PER						
TOTAL Of Lower Section	→						
TOTAL Of Upper Section	→						
GRAND TOTAL	→						

Yahtzee Score Sheet

UPPER SECTION		HOW TO SCORE	GAME #1	GAME #2	GAME #3	GAME #4	GAME #5	GAME #6
Aces	= 1	Count and Add Only Aces						
Twos	= 2	Count and Add Only Aces						
Threes	= 3	Count and Add Only Aces						
Fours	= 4	Count and Add Only Aces						
Fives	= 5	Count and Add Only Aces						
Sixes	= 6	Count and Add Only Aces						
TOTAL SCORE		→						
BONUS	If total score is 63 or over	SCORE 35						
TOTAL	Of upper Section	→						

LOWER SECTION

		HOW TO SCORE	GAME #1	GAME #2	GAME #3	GAME #4	GAME #5	GAME #6
3 of a kind		Add Total Of All Dice						
4 of a kind		Add Total Of All Dice						
Full House		SCORE 25						
Sm. Straight	Sequence of 4	SCORE 30						
Lg. Straight	Sequence of 5	SCORE 40						
YAHTZEE	of 5 a kind	SCORE 50						
Chance		Score Total Of All 5 Dice						
YAHTZEE BONUS		FOR EACH BONUS						
		SCORE 100 PER						
TOTAL	Of Lower Section	→						
TOTAL	Of Upper Section	→						
GRAND TOTAL		→						

Yahtzee Score Sheet

UPPER SECTION		HOW TO SCORE	GAME #1	GAME #2	GAME #3	GAME #4	GAME #5	GAME #6
Aces	• = 1	Count and Add Only Aces						
Twos	= 2	Count and Add Only Aces						
Threes	= 3	Count and Add Only Aces						
Fours	= 4	Count and Add Only Aces						
Fives	= 5	Count and Add Only Aces						
Sixes	= 6	Count and Add Only Aces						
TOTAL SCORE		→						
BONUS — If total score is 63 or over		SCORE 35						
TOTAL — Of upper Section		→						

LOWER SECTION

	HOW TO SCORE	GAME #1	GAME #2	GAME #3	GAME #4	GAME #5	GAME #6
3 of a kind	Add Total Of All Dice						
4 of a kind	Add Total Of All Dice						
Full House	SCORE 25						
Sm. Straight — Sequence of 4	SCORE 30						
Lg. Straight — Sequence of 5	SCORE 40						
YAHTZEE — of 5 a kind	SCORE 50						
Chance	Score Total Of All 5 Dice						
YAHTZEE BONUS	FOR EACH BONUS						
	SCORE 100 PER						
TOTAL — Of Lower Section	→						
TOTAL — Of Upper Section	→						
GRAND TOTAL	→						

Yahtzee Score Sheet

UPPER SECTION		HOW TO SCORE	GAME #1	GAME #2	GAME #3	GAME #4	GAME #5	GAME #6
Aces	• = 1	Count and Add Only Aces						
Twos	= 2	Count and Add Only Aces						
Threes	= 3	Count and Add Only Aces						
Fours	= 4	Count and Add Only Aces						
Fives	= 5	Count and Add Only Aces						
Sixes	= 6	Count and Add Only Aces						
TOTAL SCORE		→						
BONUS If total score is 63 or over		SCORE 35						
TOTAL Of upper Section		→						

LOWER SECTION

	HOW TO SCORE	GAME #1	GAME #2	GAME #3	GAME #4	GAME #5	GAME #6
3 of a kind	Add Total Of All Dice						
4 of a kind	Add Total Of All Dice						
Full House	SCORE 25						
Sm. Straight Sequence of 4	SCORE 30						
Lg. Straight Sequence of 5	SCORE 40						
YAHTZEE of 5 a kind	SCORE 50						
Chance	Score Total Of All 5 Dice						
YAHTZEE BONUS	FOR EACH BONUS						
	SCORE 100 PER						
TOTAL Of Lower Section	→						
TOTAL Of Upper Section	→						
GRAND TOTAL	→						

Yahtzee Score Sheet

UPPER SECTION		HOW TO SCORE	GAME #1	GAME #2	GAME #3	GAME #4	GAME #5	GAME #6
Aces	• = 1	Count and Add Only Aces						
Twos	•• = 2	Count and Add Only Aces						
Threes	••• = 3	Count and Add Only Aces						
Fours	•••• = 4	Count and Add Only Aces						
Fives	••••• = 5	Count and Add Only Aces						
Sixes	•••••• = 6	Count and Add Only Aces						
TOTAL SCORE		→						
BONUS — If total score is 63 or over		SCORE 35						
TOTAL — Of upper Section		→						

LOWER SECTION

		HOW TO SCORE	GAME #1	GAME #2	GAME #3	GAME #4	GAME #5	GAME #6
3 of a kind		Add Total Of All Dice						
4 of a kind		Add Total Of All Dice						
Full House		SCORE 25						
Sm. Straight	Sequence of 4	SCORE 30						
Lg. Straight	Sequence of 5	SCORE 40						
YAHTZEE	of 5 a kind	SCORE 50						
Chance		Score Total Of All 5 Dice						
YAHTZEE BONUS		FOR EACH BONUS						
		SCORE 100 PER						
TOTAL — Of Lower Section		→						
TOTAL — Of Upper Section		→						
GRAND TOTAL		→						

Yahtzee Score Sheet

UPPER SECTION		HOW TO SCORE	GAME #1	GAME #2	GAME #3	GAME #4	GAME #5	GAME #6
Aces	• = 1	Count and Add Only Aces						
Twos	•• = 2	Count and Add Only Aces						
Threes	••• = 3	Count and Add Only Aces						
Fours	•••• = 4	Count and Add Only Aces						
Fives	••••• = 5	Count and Add Only Aces						
Sixes	•••••• = 6	Count and Add Only Aces						
TOTAL SCORE		→						
BONUS	If total score is 63 or over	SCORE 35						
TOTAL	Of upper Section	→						

LOWER SECTION

		HOW TO SCORE	GAME #1	GAME #2	GAME #3	GAME #4	GAME #5	GAME #6
3 of a kind		Add Total Of All Dice						
4 of a kind		Add Total Of All Dice						
Full House		SCORE 25						
Sm. Straight	Sequence of 4	SCORE 30						
Lg. Straight	Sequence of 5	SCORE 40						
YAHTZEE	of 5 a kind	SCORE 50						
Chance		Score Total Of All 5 Dice						
YAHTZEE BONUS		FOR EACH BONUS						
		SCORE 100 PER						
TOTAL	Of Lower Section	→						
TOTAL	Of Upper Section	→						
GRAND TOTAL		→						

Yahtzee Score Sheet

UPPER SECTION	HOW TO SCORE	GAME #1	GAME #2	GAME #3	GAME #4	GAME #5	GAME #6
Aces • = 1	Count and Add Only Aces						
Twos •• = 2	Count and Add Only Aces						
Threes ••• = 3	Count and Add Only Aces						
Fours •••• = 4	Count and Add Only Aces						
Fives ••••• = 5	Count and Add Only Aces						
Sixes •••••• = 6	Count and Add Only Aces						
TOTAL SCORE	→						
BONUS If total score is 63 or over	SCORE 35						
TOTAL Of upper Section	→						

LOWER SECTION

	HOW TO SCORE	GAME #1	GAME #2	GAME #3	GAME #4	GAME #5	GAME #6
3 of a kind	Add Total Of All Dice						
4 of a kind	Add Total Of All Dice						
Full House	SCORE 25						
Sm. Straight Sequence of 4	SCORE 30						
Lg. Straight Sequence of 5	SCORE 40						
YAHTZEE of 5 a kind	SCORE 50						
Chance	Score Total Of All 5 Dice						
YAHTZEE BONUS	FOR EACH BONUS						
	SCORE 100 PER						
TOTAL Of Lower Section	→						
TOTAL Of Upper Section	→						
GRAND TOTAL	→						

Yahtzee Score Sheet

UPPER SECTION		HOW TO SCORE	GAME #1	GAME #2	GAME #3	GAME #4	GAME #5	GAME #6
Aces	• = 1	Count and Add Only Aces						
Twos	= 2	Count and Add Only Aces						
Threes	= 3	Count and Add Only Aces						
Fours	= 4	Count and Add Only Aces						
Fives	= 5	Count and Add Only Aces						
Sixes	= 6	Count and Add Only Aces						
TOTAL SCORE		→						
BONUS	If total score is 63 or over	SCORE 35						
TOTAL	Of upper Section	→						

LOWER SECTION

			GAME #1	GAME #2	GAME #3	GAME #4	GAME #5	GAME #6
3 of a kind		Add Total Of All Dice						
4 of a kind		Add Total Of All Dice						
Full House		SCORE 25						
Sm. Straight	Sequence of 4	SCORE 30						
Lg. Straight	Sequence of 5	SCORE 40						
YAHTZEE	of 5 a kind	SCORE 50						
Chance		Score Total Of All 5 Dice						
YAHTZEE BONUS		FOR EACH BONUS						
		SCORE 100 PER						
TOTAL	Of Lower Section	→						
TOTAL	Of Upper Section	→						
GRAND TOTAL		→						

Yahtzee Score Sheet

UPPER SECTION	HOW TO SCORE	GAME #1	GAME #2	GAME #3	GAME #4	GAME #5	GAME #6
Aces ● = 1	Count and Add Only Aces						
Twos ● = 2	Count and Add Only Aces						
Threes ● = 3	Count and Add Only Aces						
Fours ● = 4	Count and Add Only Aces						
Fives ● = 5	Count and Add Only Aces						
Sixes ● = 6	Count and Add Only Aces						
TOTAL SCORE	→						
BONUS — If total score is 63 or over	SCORE 35						
TOTAL — Of upper Section	→						

LOWER SECTION

LOWER SECTION	HOW TO SCORE	GAME #1	GAME #2	GAME #3	GAME #4	GAME #5	GAME #6
3 of a kind	Add Total Of All Dice						
4 of a kind	Add Total Of All Dice						
Full House	SCORE 25						
Sm. Straight — Sequence of 4	SCORE 30						
Lg. Straight — Sequence of 5	SCORE 40						
YAHTZEE — of 5 a kind	SCORE 50						
Chance	Score Total Of All 5 Dice						
YAHTZEE BONUS	FOR EACH BONUS						
YAHTZEE BONUS	SCORE 100 PER						
TOTAL — Of Lower Section	→						
TOTAL — Of Upper Section	→						
GRAND TOTAL	→						

Yahtzee Score Sheet

UPPER SECTION		HOW TO SCORE	GAME #1	GAME #2	GAME #3	GAME #4	GAME #5	GAME #6
Aces	• = 1	Count and Add Only Aces						
Twos	• = 2	Count and Add Only Aces						
Threes	• = 3	Count and Add Only Aces						
Fours	• = 4	Count and Add Only Aces						
Fives	• = 5	Count and Add Only Aces						
Sixes	• = 6	Count and Add Only Aces						
TOTAL SCORE		→						
BONUS	If total score is 63 or over	SCORE 35						
TOTAL	Of upper Section	→						

LOWER SECTION

			GAME #1	GAME #2	GAME #3	GAME #4	GAME #5	GAME #6
3 of a kind		Add Total Of All Dice						
4 of a kind		Add Total Of All Dice						
Full House		SCORE 25						
Sm. Straight	Sequence of 4	SCORE 30						
Lg. Straight	Sequence of 5	SCORE 40						
YAHTZEE	of 5 a kind	SCORE 50						
Chance		Score Total Of All 5 Dice						
YAHTZEE BONUS		FOR EACH BONUS						
		SCORE 100 PER						
TOTAL	Of Lower Section	→						
TOTAL	Of Upper Section	→						
GRAND TOTAL		→						

Yahtzee Score Sheet

UPPER SECTION		HOW TO SCORE	GAME #1	GAME #2	GAME #3	GAME #4	GAME #5	GAME #6
Aces	= 1	Count and Add Only Aces						
Twos	= 2	Count and Add Only Aces						
Threes	= 3	Count and Add Only Aces						
Fours	= 4	Count and Add Only Aces						
Fives	= 5	Count and Add Only Aces						
Sixes	= 6	Count and Add Only Aces						
TOTAL SCORE		→						
BONUS — If total score is 63 or over		SCORE 35						
TOTAL — Of upper Section		→						

LOWER SECTION

LOWER SECTION		HOW TO SCORE	GAME #1	GAME #2	GAME #3	GAME #4	GAME #5	GAME #6
3 of a kind		Add Total Of All Dice						
4 of a kind		Add Total Of All Dice						
Full House		SCORE 25						
Sm. Straight	Sequence of 4	SCORE 30						
Lg. Straight	Sequence of 5	SCORE 40						
YAHTZEE	of 5 a kind	SCORE 50						
Chance		Score Total Of All 5 Dice						
YAHTZEE BONUS		FOR EACH BONUS						
		SCORE 100 PER						
TOTAL — Of Lower Section		→						
TOTAL — Of Upper Section		→						
GRAND TOTAL		→						

Yahtzee Score Sheet

UPPER SECTION	HOW TO SCORE	GAME #1	GAME #2	GAME #3	GAME #4	GAME #5	GAME #6
Aces · = 1	Count and Add Only Aces						
Twos · = 2	Count and Add Only Aces						
Threes · = 3	Count and Add Only Aces						
Fours · = 4	Count and Add Only Aces						
Fives · = 5	Count and Add Only Aces						
Sixes · = 6	Count and Add Only Aces						
TOTAL SCORE	→						
BONUS If total score is 63 or over	SCORE 35						
TOTAL Of upper Section	→						

LOWER SECTION

LOWER SECTION	HOW TO SCORE	GAME #1	GAME #2	GAME #3	GAME #4	GAME #5	GAME #6
3 of a kind	Add Total Of All Dice						
4 of a kind	Add Total Of All Dice						
Full House	SCORE 25						
Sm. Straight Sequence of 4	SCORE 30						
Lg. Straight Sequence of 5	SCORE 40						
YAHTZEE of 5 a kind	SCORE 50						
Chance	Score Total Of All 5 Dice						
YAHTZEE BONUS	FOR EACH BONUS						
YAHTZEE BONUS	SCORE 100 PER						
TOTAL Of Lower Section	→						
TOTAL Of Upper Section	→						
GRAND TOTAL	→						

Yahtzee Score Sheet

UPPER SECTION	HOW TO SCORE	GAME #1	GAME #2	GAME #3	GAME #4	GAME #5	GAME #6
Aces ⚀ = 1	Count and Add Only Aces						
Twos ⚁ = 2	Count and Add Only Aces						
Threes ⚂ = 3	Count and Add Only Aces						
Fours ⚃ = 4	Count and Add Only Aces						
Fives ⚄ = 5	Count and Add Only Aces						
Sixes ⚅ = 6	Count and Add Only Aces						
TOTAL SCORE	→						
BONUS If total score is 63 or over	SCORE 35						
TOTAL Of upper Section	→						

LOWER SECTION

LOWER SECTION	HOW TO SCORE	GAME #1	GAME #2	GAME #3	GAME #4	GAME #5	GAME #6
3 of a kind	Add Total Of All Dice						
4 of a kind	Add Total Of All Dice						
Full House	SCORE 25						
Sm. Straight Sequence of 4	SCORE 30						
Lg. Straight Sequence of 5	SCORE 40						
YAHTZEE of 5 a kind	SCORE 50						
Chance	Score Total Of All 5 Dice						
YAHTZEE BONUS	FOR EACH BONUS						
	SCORE 100 PER						
TOTAL Of Lower Section	→						
TOTAL Of Upper Section	→						
GRAND TOTAL	→						

Yahtzee Score Sheet

UPPER SECTION			HOW TO SCORE	GAME #1	GAME #2	GAME #3	GAME #4	GAME #5	GAME #6
Aces	•	= 1	Count and Add Only Aces						
Twos		= 2	Count and Add Only Aces						
Threes		= 3	Count and Add Only Aces						
Fours		= 4	Count and Add Only Aces						
Fives		= 5	Count and Add Only Aces						
Sixes		= 6	Count and Add Only Aces						
TOTAL SCORE			→						
BONUS	If total score is 63 or over		SCORE 35						
TOTAL	Of upper Section		→						

LOWER SECTION

			HOW TO SCORE	GAME #1	GAME #2	GAME #3	GAME #4	GAME #5	GAME #6
3 of a kind			Add Total Of All Dice						
4 of a kind			Add Total Of All Dice						
Full House			SCORE 25						
Sm. Straight	Sequence of 4		SCORE 30						
Lg. Straight	Sequence of 5		SCORE 40						
YAHTZEE	of 5 a kind		SCORE 50						
Chance			Score Total Of All 5 Dice						
YAHTZEE BONUS			FOR EACH BONUS						
			SCORE 100 PER						
TOTAL	Of Lower Section		→						
TOTAL	Of Upper Section		→						
GRAND TOTAL			→						

Yahtzee Score Sheet

UPPER SECTION		HOW TO SCORE	GAME #1	GAME #2	GAME #3	GAME #4	GAME #5	GAME #6
Aces	= 1	Count and Add Only Aces						
Twos	= 2	Count and Add Only Aces						
Threes	= 3	Count and Add Only Aces						
Fours	= 4	Count and Add Only Aces						
Fives	= 5	Count and Add Only Aces						
Sixes	= 6	Count and Add Only Aces						
TOTAL SCORE		→						
BONUS	If total score is 63 or over	SCORE 35						
TOTAL	Of upper Section	→						

LOWER SECTION

			GAME #1	GAME #2	GAME #3	GAME #4	GAME #5	GAME #6
3 of a kind		Add Total Of All Dice						
4 of a kind		Add Total Of All Dice						
Full House		SCORE 25						
Sm. Straight	Sequence of 4	SCORE 30						
Lg. Straight	Sequence of 5	SCORE 40						
YAHTZEE	of 5 a kind	SCORE 50						
Chance		Score Total Of All 5 Dice						
YAHTZEE BONUS		FOR EACH BONUS						
		SCORE 100 PER						
TOTAL	Of Lower Section	→						
TOTAL	Of Upper Section	→						
GRAND TOTAL		→						

Yahtzee Score Sheet

UPPER SECTION		HOW TO SCORE	GAME #1	GAME #2	GAME #3	GAME #4	GAME #5	GAME #6
Aces	• = 1	Count and Add Only Aces						
Twos	= 2	Count and Add Only Aces						
Threes	= 3	Count and Add Only Aces						
Fours	= 4	Count and Add Only Aces						
Fives	= 5	Count and Add Only Aces						
Sixes	= 6	Count and Add Only Aces						
TOTAL SCORE		→						
BONUS	If total score is 63 or over	SCORE 35						
TOTAL	Of upper Section	→						

LOWER SECTION

		HOW TO SCORE	GAME #1	GAME #2	GAME #3	GAME #4	GAME #5	GAME #6
3 of a kind		Add Total Of All Dice						
4 of a kind		Add Total Of All Dice						
Full House		SCORE 25						
Sm. Straight	Sequence of 4	SCORE 30						
Lg. Straight	Sequence of 5	SCORE 40						
YAHTZEE	of 5 a kind	SCORE 50						
Chance		Score Total Of All 5 Dice						
YAHTZEE BONUS		FOR EACH BONUS						
		SCORE 100 PER						
TOTAL	Of Lower Section	→						
TOTAL	Of Upper Section	→						
GRAND TOTAL		→						

Yahtzee Score Sheet

UPPER SECTION		HOW TO SCORE	GAME #1	GAME #2	GAME #3	GAME #4	GAME #5	GAME #6
Aces	= 1	Count and Add Only Aces						
Twos	= 2	Count and Add Only Aces						
Threes	= 3	Count and Add Only Aces						
Fours	= 4	Count and Add Only Aces						
Fives	= 5	Count and Add Only Aces						
Sixes	= 6	Count and Add Only Aces						
TOTAL SCORE		→						
BONUS If total score is 63 or over		SCORE 35						
TOTAL Of upper Section		→						

LOWER SECTION

			GAME #1	GAME #2	GAME #3	GAME #4	GAME #5	GAME #6
3 of a kind		Add Total Of All Dice						
4 of a kind		Add Total Of All Dice						
Full House		SCORE 25						
Sm. Straight Sequence of 4		SCORE 30						
Lg. Straight Sequence of 5		SCORE 40						
YAHTZEE of 5 a kind		SCORE 50						
Chance		Score Total Of All 5 Dice						
YAHTZEE BONUS		FOR EACH BONUS						
		SCORE 100 PER						
TOTAL Of Lower Section		→						
TOTAL Of Upper Section		→						
GRAND TOTAL		→						

Yahtzee Score Sheet

UPPER SECTION		HOW TO SCORE	GAME #1	GAME #2	GAME #3	GAME #4	GAME #5	GAME #6
Aces	= 1	Count and Add Only Aces						
Twos	= 2	Count and Add Only Aces						
Threes	= 3	Count and Add Only Aces						
Fours	= 4	Count and Add Only Aces						
Fives	= 5	Count and Add Only Aces						
Sixes	= 6	Count and Add Only Aces						
TOTAL SCORE		→						
BONUS	If total score is 63 or over	SCORE 35						
TOTAL	Of upper Section	→						

LOWER SECTION

			GAME #1	GAME #2	GAME #3	GAME #4	GAME #5	GAME #6
3 of a kind		Add Total Of All Dice						
4 of a kind		Add Total Of All Dice						
Full House		SCORE 25						
Sm. Straight	Sequence of 4	SCORE 30						
Lg. Straight	Sequence of 5	SCORE 40						
YAHTZEE	of 5 a kind	SCORE 50						
Chance		Score Total Of All 5 Dice						
YAHTZEE BONUS		FOR EACH BONUS						
		SCORE 100 PER						
TOTAL	Of Lower Section	→						
TOTAL	Of Upper Section	→						
GRAND TOTAL		→						

Yahtzee Score Sheet

UPPER SECTION	HOW TO SCORE	GAME #1	GAME #2	GAME #3	GAME #4	GAME #5	GAME #6
Aces = 1	Count and Add Only Aces						
Twos = 2	Count and Add Only Aces						
Threes = 3	Count and Add Only Aces						
Fours = 4	Count and Add Only Aces						
Fives = 5	Count and Add Only Aces						
Sixes = 6	Count and Add Only Aces						
TOTAL SCORE	→						
BONUS If total score is 63 or over	SCORE 35						
TOTAL Of upper Section	→						

LOWER SECTION

	HOW TO SCORE	GAME #1	GAME #2	GAME #3	GAME #4	GAME #5	GAME #6
3 of a kind	Add Total Of All Dice						
4 of a kind	Add Total Of All Dice						
Full House	SCORE 25						
Sm. Straight Sequence of 4	SCORE 30						
Lg. Straight Sequence of 5	SCORE 40						
YAHTZEE of 5 a kind	SCORE 50						
Chance	Score Total Of All 5 Dice						
YAHTZEE BONUS	FOR EACH BONUS						
	SCORE 100 PER						
TOTAL Of Lower Section	→						
TOTAL Of Upper Section	→						
GRAND TOTAL	→						

Yahtzee Score Sheet

UPPER SECTION		HOW TO SCORE	GAME #1	GAME #2	GAME #3	GAME #4	GAME #5	GAME #6
Aces	• = 1	Count and Add Only Aces						
Twos	•• = 2	Count and Add Only Aces						
Threes	••• = 3	Count and Add Only Aces						
Fours	•••• = 4	Count and Add Only Aces						
Fives	••••• = 5	Count and Add Only Aces						
Sixes	•••••• = 6	Count and Add Only Aces						
TOTAL SCORE		→						
BONUS	If total score is 63 or over	SCORE 35						
TOTAL	Of upper Section	→						

LOWER SECTION

			GAME #1	GAME #2	GAME #3	GAME #4	GAME #5	GAME #6
3 of a kind		Add Total Of All Dice						
4 of a kind		Add Total Of All Dice						
Full House		SCORE 25						
Sm. Straight	Sequence of 4	SCORE 30						
Lg. Straight	Sequence of 5	SCORE 40						
YAHTZEE	of 5 a kind	SCORE 50						
Chance		Score Total Of All 5 Dice						
YAHTZEE BONUS		FOR EACH BONUS						
		SCORE 100 PER						
TOTAL	Of Lower Section	→						
TOTAL	Of Upper Section	→						
GRAND TOTAL		→						

Yahtzee Score Sheet

UPPER SECTION		HOW TO SCORE	GAME #1	GAME #2	GAME #3	GAME #4	GAME #5	GAME #6
Aces	= 1	Count and Add Only Aces						
Twos	= 2	Count and Add Only Aces						
Threes	= 3	Count and Add Only Aces						
Fours	= 4	Count and Add Only Aces						
Fives	= 5	Count and Add Only Aces						
Sixes	= 6	Count and Add Only Aces						
TOTAL SCORE		→						
BONUS	If total score is 63 or over	SCORE 35						
TOTAL	Of upper Section	→						

LOWER SECTION

		HOW TO SCORE	GAME #1	GAME #2	GAME #3	GAME #4	GAME #5	GAME #6
3 of a kind		Add Total Of All Dice						
4 of a kind		Add Total Of All Dice						
Full House		SCORE 25						
Sm. Straight	Sequence of 4	SCORE 30						
Lg. Straight	Sequence of 5	SCORE 40						
YAHTZEE	of 5 a kind	SCORE 50						
Chance		Score Total Of All 5 Dice						
YAHTZEE BONUS		FOR EACH BONUS						
		SCORE 100 PER						
TOTAL	Of Lower Section	→						
TOTAL	Of Upper Section	→						
GRAND TOTAL		→						

Yahtzee Score Sheet

UPPER SECTION		HOW TO SCORE	GAME #1	GAME #2	GAME #3	GAME #4	GAME #5	GAME #6
Aces	• = 1	Count and Add Only Aces						
Twos	⁚ = 2	Count and Add Only Aces						
Threes	∴ = 3	Count and Add Only Aces						
Fours	∷ = 4	Count and Add Only Aces						
Fives	⁙ = 5	Count and Add Only Aces						
Sixes	⁞⁞ = 6	Count and Add Only Aces						
TOTAL SCORE		→						
BONUS If total score is 63 or over		SCORE 35						
TOTAL Of upper Section		→						

LOWER SECTION

		HOW TO SCORE	GAME #1	GAME #2	GAME #3	GAME #4	GAME #5	GAME #6
3 of a kind		Add Total Of All Dice						
4 of a kind		Add Total Of All Dice						
Full House		SCORE 25						
Sm. Straight	Sequence of 4	SCORE 30						
Lg. Straight	Sequence of 5	SCORE 40						
YAHTZEE	of 5 a kind	SCORE 50						
Chance		Score Total Of All 5 Dice						
YAHTZEE BONUS		FOR EACH BONUS						
		SCORE 100 PER						
TOTAL Of Lower Section		→						
TOTAL Of Upper Section		→						
GRAND TOTAL		→						

Yahtzee Score Sheet

UPPER SECTION	HOW TO SCORE	GAME #1	GAME #2	GAME #3	GAME #4	GAME #5	GAME #6
Aces • = 1	Count and Add Only Aces						
Twos •• = 2	Count and Add Only Aces						
Threes ••• = 3	Count and Add Only Aces						
Fours •••• = 4	Count and Add Only Aces						
Fives ••••• = 5	Count and Add Only Aces						
Sixes •••••• = 6	Count and Add Only Aces						
TOTAL SCORE	→						
BONUS If total score is 63 or over	SCORE 35						
TOTAL Of upper Section	→						

LOWER SECTION

	HOW TO SCORE	GAME #1	GAME #2	GAME #3	GAME #4	GAME #5	GAME #6
3 of a kind	Add Total Of All Dice						
4 of a kind	Add Total Of All Dice						
Full House	SCORE 25						
Sm. Straight Sequence of 4	SCORE 30						
Lg. Straight Sequence of 5	SCORE 40						
YAHTZEE of 5 a kind	SCORE 50						
Chance	Score Total Of All 5 Dice						
YAHTZEE BONUS	FOR EACH BONUS						
	SCORE 100 PER						
TOTAL Of Lower Section	→						
TOTAL Of Upper Section	→						
GRAND TOTAL	→						

Yahtzee Score Sheet

UPPER SECTION		HOW TO SCORE	GAME #1	GAME #2	GAME #3	GAME #4	GAME #5	GAME #6
Aces	= 1	Count and Add Only Aces						
Twos	= 2	Count and Add Only Aces						
Threes	= 3	Count and Add Only Aces						
Fours	= 4	Count and Add Only Aces						
Fives	= 5	Count and Add Only Aces						
Sixes	= 6	Count and Add Only Aces						
TOTAL SCORE		→						
BONUS	If total score is 63 or over	SCORE 35						
TOTAL	Of upper Section	→						

LOWER SECTION

			GAME #1	GAME #2	GAME #3	GAME #4	GAME #5	GAME #6
3 of a kind		Add Total Of All Dice						
4 of a kind		Add Total Of All Dice						
Full House		SCORE 25						
Sm. Straight	Sequence of 4	SCORE 30						
Lg. Straight	Sequence of 5	SCORE 40						
YAHTZEE	of 5 a kind	SCORE 50						
Chance		Score Total Of All 5 Dice						
YAHTZEE BONUS		FOR EACH BONUS						
		SCORE 100 PER						
TOTAL	Of Lower Section	→						
TOTAL	Of Upper Section	→						
GRAND TOTAL		→						

Yahtzee Score Sheet

UPPER SECTION		HOW TO SCORE	GAME #1	GAME #2	GAME #3	GAME #4	GAME #5	GAME #6
Aces • = 1		Count and Add Only Aces						
Twos = 2		Count and Add Only Aces						
Threes = 3		Count and Add Only Aces						
Fours = 4		Count and Add Only Aces						
Fives = 5		Count and Add Only Aces						
Sixes = 6		Count and Add Only Aces						
TOTAL SCORE		→						
BONUS	If total score is 63 or over	SCORE 35						
TOTAL	Of upper Section	→						

LOWER SECTION

		HOW TO SCORE	GAME #1	GAME #2	GAME #3	GAME #4	GAME #5	GAME #6
3 of a kind		Add Total Of All Dice						
4 of a kind		Add Total Of All Dice						
Full House		SCORE 25						
Sm. Straight	Sequence of 4	SCORE 30						
Lg. Straight	Sequence of 5	SCORE 40						
YAHTZEE	of 5 a kind	SCORE 50						
Chance		Score Total Of All 5 Dice						
YAHTZEE BONUS		FOR EACH BONUS						
		SCORE 100 PER						
TOTAL	Of Lower Section	→						
TOTAL	Of Upper Section	→						
GRAND TOTAL		→						

Yahtzee Score Sheet

UPPER SECTION		HOW TO SCORE	GAME #1	GAME #2	GAME #3	GAME #4	GAME #5	GAME #6
Aces	• = 1	Count and Add Only Aces						
Twos	•• = 2	Count and Add Only Aces						
Threes	••• = 3	Count and Add Only Aces						
Fours	•••• = 4	Count and Add Only Aces						
Fives	••••• = 5	Count and Add Only Aces						
Sixes	•••••• = 6	Count and Add Only Aces						
TOTAL SCORE		→						
BONUS	If total score is 63 or over	SCORE 35						
TOTAL	Of upper Section	→						

LOWER SECTION

			GAME #1	GAME #2	GAME #3	GAME #4	GAME #5	GAME #6
3 of a kind		Add Total Of All Dice						
4 of a kind		Add Total Of All Dice						
Full House		SCORE 25						
Sm. Straight	Sequence of 4	SCORE 30						
Lg. Straight	Sequence of 5	SCORE 40						
YAHTZEE	of 5 a kind	SCORE 50						
Chance		Score Total Of All 5 Dice						
YAHTZEE BONUS		FOR EACH BONUS						
		SCORE 100 PER						
TOTAL	Of Lower Section	→						
TOTAL	Of Upper Section	→						
GRAND TOTAL		→						

Yahtzee Score Sheet

UPPER SECTION		HOW TO SCORE	GAME #1	GAME #2	GAME #3	GAME #4	GAME #5	GAME #6
Aces	= 1	Count and Add Only Aces						
Twos	= 2	Count and Add Only Aces						
Threes	= 3	Count and Add Only Aces						
Fours	= 4	Count and Add Only Aces						
Fives	= 5	Count and Add Only Aces						
Sixes	= 6	Count and Add Only Aces						
TOTAL SCORE		→						
BONUS	If total score is 63 or over	SCORE 35						
TOTAL	Of upper Section	→						

LOWER SECTION

	HOW TO SCORE	GAME #1	GAME #2	GAME #3	GAME #4	GAME #5	GAME #6
3 of a kind	Add Total Of All Dice						
4 of a kind	Add Total Of All Dice						
Full House	SCORE 25						
Sm. Straight — Sequence of 4	SCORE 30						
Lg. Straight — Sequence of 5	SCORE 40						
YAHTZEE — of 5 a kind	SCORE 50						
Chance	Score Total Of All 5 Dice						
YAHTZEE BONUS	FOR EACH BONUS						
YAHTZEE BONUS	SCORE 100 PER						
TOTAL — Of Lower Section	→						
TOTAL — Of Upper Section	→						
GRAND TOTAL	→						

Yahtzee Score Sheet

UPPER SECTION		HOW TO SCORE	GAME #1	GAME #2	GAME #3	GAME #4	GAME #5	GAME #6
Aces	• = 1	Count and Add Only Aces						
Twos	= 2	Count and Add Only Aces						
Threes	= 3	Count and Add Only Aces						
Fours	= 4	Count and Add Only Aces						
Fives	= 5	Count and Add Only Aces						
Sixes	= 6	Count and Add Only Aces						
TOTAL SCORE		→						
BONUS	If total score is 63 or over	SCORE 35						
TOTAL	Of upper Section	→						

LOWER SECTION

			GAME #1	GAME #2	GAME #3	GAME #4	GAME #5	GAME #6
3 of a kind		Add Total Of All Dice						
4 of a kind		Add Total Of All Dice						
Full House		SCORE 25						
Sm. Straight	Sequence of 4	SCORE 30						
Lg. Straight	Sequence of 5	SCORE 40						
YAHTZEE	of 5 a kind	SCORE 50						
Chance		Score Total Of All 5 Dice						
YAHTZEE BONUS		FOR EACH BONUS						
		SCORE 100 PER						
TOTAL	Of Lower Section	→						
TOTAL	Of Upper Section	→						
GRAND TOTAL		→						

Yahtzee Score Sheet

UPPER SECTION		HOW TO SCORE	GAME #1	GAME #2	GAME #3	GAME #4	GAME #5	GAME #6
Aces	• = 1	Count and Add Only Aces						
Twos	= 2	Count and Add Only Aces						
Threes	= 3	Count and Add Only Aces						
Fours	= 4	Count and Add Only Aces						
Fives	= 5	Count and Add Only Aces						
Sixes	= 6	Count and Add Only Aces						
TOTAL SCORE		→						
BONUS	If total score is 63 or over	SCORE 35						
TOTAL	Of upper Section	→						

LOWER SECTION

			GAME #1	GAME #2	GAME #3	GAME #4	GAME #5	GAME #6
3 of a kind		Add Total Of All Dice						
4 of a kind		Add Total Of All Dice						
Full House		SCORE 25						
Sm. Straight	Sequence of 4	SCORE 30						
Lg. Straight	Sequence of 5	SCORE 40						
YAHTZEE	of 5 a kind	SCORE 50						
Chance		Score Total Of All 5 Dice						
YAHTZEE BONUS		FOR EACH BONUS						
		SCORE 100 PER						
TOTAL	Of Lower Section	→						
TOTAL	Of Upper Section	→						
GRAND TOTAL		→						

Yahtzee Score Sheet

UPPER SECTION		HOW TO SCORE	GAME #1	GAME #2	GAME #3	GAME #4	GAME #5	GAME #6
Aces	● = 1	Count and Add Only Aces						
Twos	= 2	Count and Add Only Aces						
Threes	= 3	Count and Add Only Aces						
Fours	= 4	Count and Add Only Aces						
Fives	= 5	Count and Add Only Aces						
Sixes	= 6	Count and Add Only Aces						
TOTAL SCORE		→						
BONUS	If total score is 63 or over	SCORE 35						
TOTAL	Of upper Section	→						

LOWER SECTION

			GAME #1	GAME #2	GAME #3	GAME #4	GAME #5	GAME #6
3 of a kind		Add Total Of All Dice						
4 of a kind		Add Total Of All Dice						
Full House		SCORE 25						
Sm. Straight	Sequence of 4	SCORE 30						
Lg. Straight	Sequence of 5	SCORE 40						
YAHTZEE	of 5 a kind	SCORE 50						
Chance		Score Total Of All 5 Dice						
YAHTZEE BONUS		FOR EACH BONUS						
		SCORE 100 PER						
TOTAL	Of Lower Section	→						
TOTAL	Of Upper Section	→						
GRAND TOTAL		→						

Yahtzee Score Sheet

UPPER SECTION		HOW TO SCORE	GAME #1	GAME #2	GAME #3	GAME #4	GAME #5	GAME #6
Aces	= 1	Count and Add Only Aces						
Twos	= 2	Count and Add Only Aces						
Threes	= 3	Count and Add Only Aces						
Fours	= 4	Count and Add Only Aces						
Fives	= 5	Count and Add Only Aces						
Sixes	= 6	Count and Add Only Aces						
TOTAL SCORE		→						
BONUS	If total score is 63 or over	SCORE 35						
TOTAL	Of upper Section	→						

LOWER SECTION

		HOW TO SCORE	GAME #1	GAME #2	GAME #3	GAME #4	GAME #5	GAME #6
3 of a kind		Add Total Of All Dice						
4 of a kind		Add Total Of All Dice						
Full House		SCORE 25						
Sm. Straight	Sequence of 4	SCORE 30						
Lg. Straight	Sequence of 5	SCORE 40						
YAHTZEE	of 5 a kind	SCORE 50						
Chance		Score Total Of All 5 Dice						
YAHTZEE BONUS		FOR EACH BONUS						
		SCORE 100 PER						
TOTAL	Of Lower Section	→						
TOTAL	Of Upper Section	→						
GRAND TOTAL		→						

Yahtzee Score Sheet

UPPER SECTION	HOW TO SCORE	GAME #1	GAME #2	GAME #3	GAME #4	GAME #5	GAME #6
Aces = 1	Count and Add Only Aces						
Twos = 2	Count and Add Only Aces						
Threes = 3	Count and Add Only Aces						
Fours = 4	Count and Add Only Aces						
Fives = 5	Count and Add Only Aces						
Sixes = 6	Count and Add Only Aces						
TOTAL SCORE	→						
BONUS If total score is 63 or over	SCORE 35						
TOTAL Of upper Section	→						

LOWER SECTION

	HOW TO SCORE	GAME #1	GAME #2	GAME #3	GAME #4	GAME #5	GAME #6
3 of a kind	Add Total Of All Dice						
4 of a kind	Add Total Of All Dice						
Full House	SCORE 25						
Sm. Straight Sequence of 4	SCORE 30						
Lg. Straight Sequence of 5	SCORE 40						
YAHTZEE of 5 a kind	SCORE 50						
Chance	Score Total Of All 5 Dice						
YAHTZEE BONUS	FOR EACH BONUS						
	SCORE 100 PER						
TOTAL Of Lower Section	→						
TOTAL Of Upper Section	→						
GRAND TOTAL	→						

Yahtzee Score Sheet

UPPER SECTION		HOW TO SCORE	GAME #1	GAME #2	GAME #3	GAME #4	GAME #5	GAME #6
Aces	= 1	Count and Add Only Aces						
Twos	= 2	Count and Add Only Aces						
Threes	= 3	Count and Add Only Aces						
Fours	= 4	Count and Add Only Aces						
Fives	= 5	Count and Add Only Aces						
Sixes	= 6	Count and Add Only Aces						
TOTAL SCORE		→						
BONUS If total score is 63 or over		SCORE 35						
TOTAL Of upper Section		→						

LOWER SECTION

			GAME #1	GAME #2	GAME #3	GAME #4	GAME #5	GAME #6
3 of a kind		Add Total Of All Dice						
4 of a kind		Add Total Of All Dice						
Full House		SCORE 25						
Sm. Straight	Sequence of 4	SCORE 30						
Lg. Straight	Sequence of 5	SCORE 40						
YAHTZEE	of 5 a kind	SCORE 50						
Chance		Score Total Of All 5 Dice						
YAHTZEE BONUS		FOR EACH BONUS						
		SCORE 100 PER						
TOTAL Of Lower Section		→						
TOTAL Of Upper Section		→						
GRAND TOTAL		→						

Yahtzee Score Sheet

UPPER SECTION		HOW TO SCORE	GAME #1	GAME #2	GAME #3	GAME #4	GAME #5	GAME #6
Aces	= 1	Count and Add Only Aces						
Twos	= 2	Count and Add Only Aces						
Threes	= 3	Count and Add Only Aces						
Fours	= 4	Count and Add Only Aces						
Fives	= 5	Count and Add Only Aces						
Sixes	= 6	Count and Add Only Aces						
TOTAL SCORE		→						
BONUS If total score is 63 or over		SCORE 35						
TOTAL Of upper Section		→						

LOWER SECTION

		HOW TO SCORE	GAME #1	GAME #2	GAME #3	GAME #4	GAME #5	GAME #6
3 of a kind		Add Total Of All Dice						
4 of a kind		Add Total Of All Dice						
Full House		SCORE 25						
Sm. Straight	Sequence of 4	SCORE 30						
Lg. Straight	Sequence of 5	SCORE 40						
YAHTZEE	of 5 a kind	SCORE 50						
Chance		Score Total Of All 5 Dice						
YAHTZEE BONUS		FOR EACH BONUS						
		SCORE 100 PER						
TOTAL Of Lower Section		→						
TOTAL Of Upper Section		→						
GRAND TOTAL		→						

Yahtzee Score Sheet

UPPER SECTION		HOW TO SCORE	GAME #1	GAME #2	GAME #3	GAME #4	GAME #5	GAME #6
Aces	= 1	Count and Add Only Aces						
Twos	= 2	Count and Add Only Aces						
Threes	= 3	Count and Add Only Aces						
Fours	= 4	Count and Add Only Aces						
Fives	= 5	Count and Add Only Aces						
Sixes	= 6	Count and Add Only Aces						
TOTAL SCORE		→						
BONUS	If total score is 63 or over	SCORE 35						
TOTAL	Of upper Section	→						

LOWER SECTION

		HOW TO SCORE	GAME #1	GAME #2	GAME #3	GAME #4	GAME #5	GAME #6
3 of a kind		Add Total Of All Dice						
4 of a kind		Add Total Of All Dice						
Full House		SCORE 25						
Sm. Straight	Sequence of 4	SCORE 30						
Lg. Straight	Sequence of 5	SCORE 40						
YAHTZEE	of 5 a kind	SCORE 50						
Chance		Score Total Of All 5 Dice						
YAHTZEE BONUS		FOR EACH BONUS						
		SCORE 100 PER						
TOTAL	Of Lower Section	→						
TOTAL	Of Upper Section	→						
GRAND TOTAL		→						

Yahtzee Score Sheet

UPPER SECTION	HOW TO SCORE	GAME #1	GAME #2	GAME #3	GAME #4	GAME #5	GAME #6
Aces • = 1	Count and Add Only Aces						
Twos = 2	Count and Add Only Aces						
Threes = 3	Count and Add Only Aces						
Fours = 4	Count and Add Only Aces						
Fives = 5	Count and Add Only Aces						
Sixes = 6	Count and Add Only Aces						
TOTAL SCORE	→						
BONUS If total score is 63 or over	SCORE 35						
TOTAL Of upper Section	→						

LOWER SECTION

LOWER SECTION	HOW TO SCORE	GAME #1	GAME #2	GAME #3	GAME #4	GAME #5	GAME #6
3 of a kind	Add Total Of All Dice						
4 of a kind	Add Total Of All Dice						
Full House	SCORE 25						
Sm. Straight Sequence of 4	SCORE 30						
Lg. Straight Sequence of 5	SCORE 40						
YAHTZEE of 5 a kind	SCORE 50						
Chance	Score Total Of All 5 Dice						
YAHTZEE BONUS	FOR EACH BONUS						
	SCORE 100 PER						
TOTAL Of Lower Section	→						
TOTAL Of Upper Section	→						
GRAND TOTAL	→						

Yahtzee Score Sheet

UPPER SECTION		HOW TO SCORE	GAME #1	GAME #2	GAME #3	GAME #4	GAME #5	GAME #6
Aces	• = 1	Count and Add Only Aces						
Twos	= 2	Count and Add Only Aces						
Threes	= 3	Count and Add Only Aces						
Fours	= 4	Count and Add Only Aces						
Fives	= 5	Count and Add Only Aces						
Sixes	= 6	Count and Add Only Aces						
TOTAL SCORE		→						
BONUS	If total score is 63 or over	SCORE 35						
TOTAL	Of upper Section	→						

LOWER SECTION

			GAME #1	GAME #2	GAME #3	GAME #4	GAME #5	GAME #6
3 of a kind		Add Total Of All Dice						
4 of a kind		Add Total Of All Dice						
Full House		SCORE 25						
Sm. Straight	Sequence of 4	SCORE 30						
Lg. Straight	Sequence of 5	SCORE 40						
YAHTZEE	of 5 a kind	SCORE 50						
Chance		Score Total Of All 5 Dice						
YAHTZEE BONUS		FOR EACH BONUS						
		SCORE 100 PER						
TOTAL	Of Lower Section	→						
TOTAL	Of Upper Section	→						
GRAND TOTAL		→						

Yahtzee Score Sheet

UPPER SECTION		HOW TO SCORE	GAME #1	GAME #2	GAME #3	GAME #4	GAME #5	GAME #6
Aces	= 1	Count and Add Only Aces						
Twos	= 2	Count and Add Only Aces						
Threes	= 3	Count and Add Only Aces						
Fours	= 4	Count and Add Only Aces						
Fives	= 5	Count and Add Only Aces						
Sixes	= 6	Count and Add Only Aces						
TOTAL SCORE		→						
BONUS	If total score is 63 or over	SCORE 35						
TOTAL	Of upper Section	→						

LOWER SECTION

		HOW TO SCORE	GAME #1	GAME #2	GAME #3	GAME #4	GAME #5	GAME #6
3 of a kind		Add Total Of All Dice						
4 of a kind		Add Total Of All Dice						
Full House		SCORE 25						
Sm. Straight	Sequence of 4	SCORE 30						
Lg. Straight	Sequence of 5	SCORE 40						
YAHTZEE	of 5 a kind	SCORE 50						
Chance		Score Total Of All 5 Dice						
YAHTZEE BONUS		FOR EACH BONUS						
		SCORE 100 PER						
TOTAL	Of Lower Section	→						
TOTAL	Of Upper Section	→						
GRAND TOTAL		→						

Yahtzee Score Sheet

UPPER SECTION		HOW TO SCORE	GAME #1	GAME #2	GAME #3	GAME #4	GAME #5	GAME #6
Aces	• = 1	Count and Add Only Aces						
Twos	= 2	Count and Add Only Aces						
Threes	= 3	Count and Add Only Aces						
Fours	= 4	Count and Add Only Aces						
Fives	= 5	Count and Add Only Aces						
Sixes	= 6	Count and Add Only Aces						
TOTAL SCORE		→						
BONUS	If total score is 63 or over	SCORE 35						
TOTAL	Of upper Section	→						

LOWER SECTION

		HOW TO SCORE	GAME #1	GAME #2	GAME #3	GAME #4	GAME #5	GAME #6
3 of a kind		Add Total Of All Dice						
4 of a kind		Add Total Of All Dice						
Full House		SCORE 25						
Sm. Straight	Sequence of 4	SCORE 30						
Lg. Straight	Sequence of 5	SCORE 40						
YAHTZEE	of 5 a kind	SCORE 50						
Chance		Score Total Of All 5 Dice						
YAHTZEE BONUS		FOR EACH BONUS						
		SCORE 100 PER						
TOTAL	Of Lower Section	→						
TOTAL	Of Upper Section	→						
GRAND TOTAL		→						

Yahtzee Score Sheet

UPPER SECTION		HOW TO SCORE	GAME #1	GAME #2	GAME #3	GAME #4	GAME #5	GAME #6
Aces	• = 1	Count and Add Only Aces						
Twos	= 2	Count and Add Only Aces						
Threes	= 3	Count and Add Only Aces						
Fours	= 4	Count and Add Only Aces						
Fives	= 5	Count and Add Only Aces						
Sixes	= 6	Count and Add Only Aces						
TOTAL SCORE		→						
BONUS If total score is 63 or over		SCORE 35						
TOTAL Of upper Section		→						

LOWER SECTION

LOWER SECTION		HOW TO SCORE	GAME #1	GAME #2	GAME #3	GAME #4	GAME #5	GAME #6
3 of a kind		Add Total Of All Dice						
4 of a kind		Add Total Of All Dice						
Full House		SCORE 25						
Sm. Straight	Sequence of 4	SCORE 30						
Lg. Straight	Sequence of 5	SCORE 40						
YAHTZEE	of 5 a kind	SCORE 50						
Chance		Score Total Of All 5 Dice						
YAHTZEE BONUS		FOR EACH BONUS						
		SCORE 100 PER						
TOTAL Of Lower Section		→						
TOTAL Of Upper Section		→						
GRAND TOTAL		→						

Yahtzee Score Sheet

UPPER SECTION		HOW TO SCORE	GAME #1	GAME #2	GAME #3	GAME #4	GAME #5	GAME #6
Aces	= 1	Count and Add Only Aces						
Twos	= 2	Count and Add Only Aces						
Threes	= 3	Count and Add Only Aces						
Fours	= 4	Count and Add Only Aces						
Fives	= 5	Count and Add Only Aces						
Sixes	= 6	Count and Add Only Aces						
TOTAL SCORE		→						
BONUS If total score is 63 or over		SCORE 35						
TOTAL Of upper Section		→						

LOWER SECTION

	HOW TO SCORE	GAME #1	GAME #2	GAME #3	GAME #4	GAME #5	GAME #6
3 of a kind	Add Total Of All Dice						
4 of a kind	Add Total Of All Dice						
Full House	SCORE 25						
Sm. Straight Sequence of 4	SCORE 30						
Lg. Straight Sequence of 5	SCORE 40						
YAHTZEE of 5 a kind	SCORE 50						
Chance	Score Total Of All 5 Dice						
YAHTZEE BONUS	FOR EACH BONUS						
	SCORE 100 PER						
TOTAL Of Lower Section	→						
TOTAL Of Upper Section	→						
GRAND TOTAL	→						

Yahtzee Score Sheet

UPPER SECTION		HOW TO SCORE	GAME #1	GAME #2	GAME #3	GAME #4	GAME #5	GAME #6
Aces	$\bullet$ = 1	Count and Add Only Aces						
Twos	= 2	Count and Add Only Aces						
Threes	= 3	Count and Add Only Aces						
Fours	= 4	Count and Add Only Aces						
Fives	= 5	Count and Add Only Aces						
Sixes	= 6	Count and Add Only Aces						
TOTAL SCORE		$\longrightarrow$						
BONUS	If total score is 63 or over	SCORE 35						
TOTAL	Of upper Section	$\longrightarrow$						

LOWER SECTION

			GAME #1	GAME #2	GAME #3	GAME #4	GAME #5	GAME #6
3 of a kind		Add Total Of All Dice						
4 of a kind		Add Total Of All Dice						
Full House		SCORE 25						
Sm. Straight	Sequence of 4	SCORE 30						
Lg. Straight	Sequence of 5	SCORE 40						
YAHTZEE	of 5 a kind	SCORE 50						
Chance		Score Total Of All 5 Dice						
YAHTZEE BONUS		FOR EACH BONUS						
		SCORE 100 PER						
TOTAL	Of Lower Section	$\longrightarrow$						
TOTAL	Of Upper Section	$\longrightarrow$						
GRAND TOTAL		$\longrightarrow$						

Yahtzee Score Sheet

UPPER SECTION		HOW TO SCORE	GAME #1	GAME #2	GAME #3	GAME #4	GAME #5	GAME #6
Aces	$\bullet$ = 1	Count and Add Only Aces						
Twos	= 2	Count and Add Only Aces						
Threes	= 3	Count and Add Only Aces						
Fours	= 4	Count and Add Only Aces						
Fives	= 5	Count and Add Only Aces						
Sixes	= 6	Count and Add Only Aces						
TOTAL SCORE		→						
BONUS	If total score is 63 or over	SCORE 35						
TOTAL	Of upper Section	→						

LOWER SECTION

			GAME #1	GAME #2	GAME #3	GAME #4	GAME #5	GAME #6
3 of a kind		Add Total Of All Dice						
4 of a kind		Add Total Of All Dice						
Full House		SCORE 25						
Sm. Straight	Sequence of 4	SCORE 30						
Lg. Straight	Sequence of 5	SCORE 40						
YAHTZEE	of 5 a kind	SCORE 50						
Chance		Score Total Of All 5 Dice						
YAHTZEE BONUS		FOR EACH BONUS						
		SCORE 100 PER						
TOTAL	Of Lower Section	→						
TOTAL	Of Upper Section	→						
GRAND TOTAL		→						

Yahtzee Score Sheet

UPPER SECTION	HOW TO SCORE	GAME #1	GAME #2	GAME #3	GAME #4	GAME #5	GAME #6
Aces ⚀ = 1	Count and Add Only Aces						
Twos ⚁ = 2	Count and Add Only Aces						
Threes ⚂ = 3	Count and Add Only Aces						
Fours ⚃ = 4	Count and Add Only Aces						
Fives ⚄ = 5	Count and Add Only Aces						
Sixes ⚅ = 6	Count and Add Only Aces						
TOTAL SCORE	→						
BONUS If total score is 63 or over	SCORE 35						
TOTAL Of upper Section	→						

LOWER SECTION

	HOW TO SCORE	GAME #1	GAME #2	GAME #3	GAME #4	GAME #5	GAME #6
3 of a kind	Add Total Of All Dice						
4 of a kind	Add Total Of All Dice						
Full House	SCORE 25						
Sm. Straight Sequence of 4	SCORE 30						
Lg. Straight Sequence of 5	SCORE 40						
YAHTZEE of 5 a kind	SCORE 50						
Chance	Score Total Of All 5 Dice						
YAHTZEE BONUS	FOR EACH BONUS						
	SCORE 100 PER						
TOTAL Of Lower Section	→						
TOTAL Of Upper Section	→						
GRAND TOTAL	→						

Yahtzee Score Sheet

UPPER SECTION		HOW TO SCORE	GAME #1	GAME #2	GAME #3	GAME #4	GAME #5	GAME #6
Aces	= 1	Count and Add Only Aces						
Twos	= 2	Count and Add Only Aces						
Threes	= 3	Count and Add Only Aces						
Fours	= 4	Count and Add Only Aces						
Fives	= 5	Count and Add Only Aces						
Sixes	= 6	Count and Add Only Aces						
TOTAL SCORE		→						
BONUS If total score is 63 or over		SCORE 35						
TOTAL Of upper Section		→						

LOWER SECTION

		HOW TO SCORE	GAME #1	GAME #2	GAME #3	GAME #4	GAME #5	GAME #6
3 of a kind		Add Total Of All Dice						
4 of a kind		Add Total Of All Dice						
Full House		SCORE 25						
Sm. Straight	Sequence of 4	SCORE 30						
Lg. Straight	Sequence of 5	SCORE 40						
YAHTZEE	of 5 a kind	SCORE 50						
Chance		Score Total Of All 5 Dice						
YAHTZEE BONUS		FOR EACH BONUS						
		SCORE 100 PER						
TOTAL	Of Lower Section	→						
TOTAL	Of Upper Section	→						
GRAND TOTAL		→						

Yahtzee Score Sheet

UPPER SECTION	HOW TO SCORE	GAME #1	GAME #2	GAME #3	GAME #4	GAME #5	GAME #6
Aces ● = 1	Count and Add Only Aces						
Twos ⚁ = 2	Count and Add Only Aces						
Threes ⚂ = 3	Count and Add Only Aces						
Fours ⚃ = 4	Count and Add Only Aces						
Fives ⚄ = 5	Count and Add Only Aces						
Sixes ⚅ = 6	Count and Add Only Aces						
TOTAL SCORE	→						
BONUS If total score is 63 or over	SCORE 35						
TOTAL Of upper Section	→						

LOWER SECTION

	HOW TO SCORE	GAME #1	GAME #2	GAME #3	GAME #4	GAME #5	GAME #6
3 of a kind	Add Total Of All Dice						
4 of a kind	Add Total Of All Dice						
Full House	SCORE 25						
Sm. Straight Sequence of 4	SCORE 30						
Lg. Straight Sequence of 5	SCORE 40						
YAHTZEE of 5 a kind	SCORE 50						
Chance	Score Total Of All 5 Dice						
YAHTZEE BONUS	FOR EACH BONUS						
	SCORE 100 PER						
TOTAL Of Lower Section	→						
TOTAL Of Upper Section	→						
GRAND TOTAL	→						

Yahtzee Score Sheet

UPPER SECTION		HOW TO SCORE	GAME #1	GAME #2	GAME #3	GAME #4	GAME #5	GAME #6
Aces	• = 1	Count and Add Only Aces						
Twos	= 2	Count and Add Only Aces						
Threes	= 3	Count and Add Only Aces						
Fours	= 4	Count and Add Only Aces						
Fives	= 5	Count and Add Only Aces						
Sixes	= 6	Count and Add Only Aces						
TOTAL SCORE		→						
BONUS	If total score is 63 or over	SCORE 35						
TOTAL	Of upper Section	→						

LOWER SECTION

		HOW TO SCORE	GAME #1	GAME #2	GAME #3	GAME #4	GAME #5	GAME #6
3 of a kind		Add Total Of All Dice						
4 of a kind		Add Total Of All Dice						
Full House		SCORE 25						
Sm. Straight	Sequence of 4	SCORE 30						
Lg. Straight	Sequence of 5	SCORE 40						
YAHTZEE	of 5 a kind	SCORE 50						
Chance		Score Total Of All 5 Dice						
YAHTZEE BONUS		FOR EACH BONUS						
		SCORE 100 PER						
TOTAL	Of Lower Section	→						
TOTAL	Of Upper Section	→						
GRAND TOTAL		→						

Yahtzee Score Sheet

UPPER SECTION		HOW TO SCORE	GAME #1	GAME #2	GAME #3	GAME #4	GAME #5	GAME #6
Aces	• = 1	Count and Add Only Aces						
Twos	•• = 2	Count and Add Only Aces						
Threes	••• = 3	Count and Add Only Aces						
Fours	•••• = 4	Count and Add Only Aces						
Fives	••••• = 5	Count and Add Only Aces						
Sixes	•••••• = 6	Count and Add Only Aces						
TOTAL SCORE		→						
BONUS	If total score is 63 or over	SCORE 35						
TOTAL	Of upper Section	→						

LOWER SECTION

			GAME #1	GAME #2	GAME #3	GAME #4	GAME #5	GAME #6
3 of a kind		Add Total Of All Dice						
4 of a kind		Add Total Of All Dice						
Full House		SCORE 25						
Sm. Straight	Sequence of 4	SCORE 30						
Lg. Straight	Sequence of 5	SCORE 40						
YAHTZEE	of 5 a kind	SCORE 50						
Chance		Score Total Of All 5 Dice						
YAHTZEE BONUS		FOR EACH BONUS						
		SCORE 100 PER						
TOTAL	Of Lower Section	→						
TOTAL	Of Upper Section	→						
GRAND TOTAL		→						

Yahtzee Score Sheet

UPPER SECTION		HOW TO SCORE	GAME #1	GAME #2	GAME #3	GAME #4	GAME #5	GAME #6
Aces	= 1	Count and Add Only Aces						
Twos	= 2	Count and Add Only Aces						
Threes	= 3	Count and Add Only Aces						
Fours	= 4	Count and Add Only Aces						
Fives	= 5	Count and Add Only Aces						
Sixes	= 6	Count and Add Only Aces						
TOTAL SCORE		→						
BONUS	If total score is 63 or over	SCORE 35						
TOTAL	Of upper Section	→						

LOWER SECTION

		HOW TO SCORE	GAME #1	GAME #2	GAME #3	GAME #4	GAME #5	GAME #6
3 of a kind		Add Total Of All Dice						
4 of a kind		Add Total Of All Dice						
Full House		SCORE 25						
Sm. Straight	Sequence of 4	SCORE 30						
Lg. Straight	Sequence of 5	SCORE 40						
YAHTZEE	of 5 a kind	SCORE 50						
Chance		Score Total Of All 5 Dice						
YAHTZEE BONUS		FOR EACH BONUS						
		SCORE 100 PER						
TOTAL	Of Lower Section	→						
TOTAL	Of Upper Section	→						
GRAND TOTAL		→						

Yahtzee Score Sheet

UPPER SECTION		HOW TO SCORE	GAME #1	GAME #2	GAME #3	GAME #4	GAME #5	GAME #6
Aces	• = 1	Count and Add Only Aces						
Twos	•• = 2	Count and Add Only Aces						
Threes	••• = 3	Count and Add Only Aces						
Fours	•••• = 4	Count and Add Only Aces						
Fives	••••• = 5	Count and Add Only Aces						
Sixes	•••••• = 6	Count and Add Only Aces						
TOTAL SCORE		→						
BONUS — If total score is 63 or over		SCORE 35						
TOTAL — Of upper Section		→						

LOWER SECTION

		HOW TO SCORE	GAME #1	GAME #2	GAME #3	GAME #4	GAME #5	GAME #6
3 of a kind		Add Total Of All Dice						
4 of a kind		Add Total Of All Dice						
Full House		SCORE 25						
Sm. Straight	Sequence of 4	SCORE 30						
Lg. Straight	Sequence of 5	SCORE 40						
YAHTZEE	of 5 a kind	SCORE 50						
Chance		Score Total Of All 5 Dice						
YAHTZEE BONUS		FOR EACH BONUS						
		SCORE 100 PER						
TOTAL — Of Lower Section		→						
TOTAL — Of Upper Section		→						
GRAND TOTAL		→						

Yahtzee Score Sheet

UPPER SECTION		HOW TO SCORE	GAME #1	GAME #2	GAME #3	GAME #4	GAME #5	GAME #6
Aces	= 1	Count and Add Only Aces						
Twos	= 2	Count and Add Only Aces						
Threes	= 3	Count and Add Only Aces						
Fours	= 4	Count and Add Only Aces						
Fives	= 5	Count and Add Only Aces						
Sixes	= 6	Count and Add Only Aces						
TOTAL SCORE		→						
BONUS	If total score is 63 or over	SCORE 35						
TOTAL	Of upper Section	→						

LOWER SECTION

			GAME #1	GAME #2	GAME #3	GAME #4	GAME #5	GAME #6
3 of a kind		Add Total Of All Dice						
4 of a kind		Add Total Of All Dice						
Full House		SCORE 25						
Sm. Straight	Sequence of 4	SCORE 30						
Lg. Straight	Sequence of 5	SCORE 40						
YAHTZEE	of 5 a kind	SCORE 50						
Chance		Score Total Of All 5 Dice						
YAHTZEE BONUS		FOR EACH BONUS						
		SCORE 100 PER						
TOTAL	Of Lower Section	→						
TOTAL	Of Upper Section	→						
GRAND TOTAL		→						

Yahtzee Score Sheet

UPPER SECTION			HOW TO SCORE	GAME #1	GAME #2	GAME #3	GAME #4	GAME #5	GAME #6
Aces		= 1	Count and Add Only Aces						
Twos		= 2	Count and Add Only Aces						
Threes		= 3	Count and Add Only Aces						
Fours		= 4	Count and Add Only Aces						
Fives		= 5	Count and Add Only Aces						
Sixes		= 6	Count and Add Only Aces						
TOTAL SCORE			→						
BONUS	If total score is 63 or over		SCORE 35						
TOTAL	Of upper Section		→						

LOWER SECTION

			HOW TO SCORE	GAME #1	GAME #2	GAME #3	GAME #4	GAME #5	GAME #6
3 of a kind			Add Total Of All Dice						
4 of a kind			Add Total Of All Dice						
Full House			SCORE 25						
Sm. Straight	Sequence of 4		SCORE 30						
Lg. Straight	Sequence of 5		SCORE 40						
YAHTZEE	of 5 a kind		SCORE 50						
Chance			Score Total Of All 5 Dice						
YAHTZEE BONUS			FOR EACH BONUS						
			SCORE 100 PER						
TOTAL	Of Lower Section		→						
TOTAL	Of Upper Section		→						
GRAND TOTAL			→						

Yahtzee Score Sheet

UPPER SECTION		HOW TO SCORE	GAME #1	GAME #2	GAME #3	GAME #4	GAME #5	GAME #6
Aces	• = 1	Count and Add Only Aces						
Twos	• = 2	Count and Add Only Aces						
Threes	• = 3	Count and Add Only Aces						
Fours	• = 4	Count and Add Only Aces						
Fives	• = 5	Count and Add Only Aces						
Sixes	• = 6	Count and Add Only Aces						
TOTAL SCORE		→						
BONUS If total score is 63 or over		SCORE 35						
TOTAL Of upper Section		→						

LOWER SECTION

		HOW TO SCORE	GAME #1	GAME #2	GAME #3	GAME #4	GAME #5	GAME #6
3 of a kind		Add Total Of All Dice						
4 of a kind		Add Total Of All Dice						
Full House		SCORE 25						
Sm. Straight	Sequence of 4	SCORE 30						
Lg. Straight	Sequence of 5	SCORE 40						
YAHTZEE	of 5 a kind	SCORE 50						
Chance		Score Total Of All 5 Dice						
YAHTZEE BONUS		FOR EACH BONUS						
		SCORE 100 PER						
TOTAL Of Lower Section		→						
TOTAL Of Upper Section		→						
GRAND TOTAL		→						

Yahtzee Score Sheet

UPPER SECTION	HOW TO SCORE	GAME #1	GAME #2	GAME #3	GAME #4	GAME #5	GAME #6
Aces • = 1	Count and Add Only Aces						
Twos •• = 2	Count and Add Only Aces						
Threes ••• = 3	Count and Add Only Aces						
Fours •• = 4	Count and Add Only Aces						
Fives ••• = 5	Count and Add Only Aces						
Sixes ••• = 6	Count and Add Only Aces						
TOTAL SCORE	→						
BONUS If total score is 63 or over	SCORE 35						
TOTAL Of upper Section	→						

LOWER SECTION

	HOW TO SCORE	GAME #1	GAME #2	GAME #3	GAME #4	GAME #5	GAME #6
3 of a kind	Add Total Of All Dice						
4 of a kind	Add Total Of All Dice						
Full House	SCORE 25						
Sm. Straight Sequence of 4	SCORE 30						
Lg. Straight Sequence of 5	SCORE 40						
YAHTZEE of 5 a kind	SCORE 50						
Chance	Score Total Of All 5 Dice						
YAHTZEE BONUS	FOR EACH BONUS						
	SCORE 100 PER						
TOTAL Of Lower Section	→						
TOTAL Of Upper Section	→						
GRAND TOTAL	→						

Yahtzee Score Sheet

UPPER SECTION		HOW TO SCORE	GAME #1	GAME #2	GAME #3	GAME #4	GAME #5	GAME #6
Aces	• = 1	Count and Add Only Aces						
Twos	= 2	Count and Add Only Aces						
Threes	= 3	Count and Add Only Aces						
Fours	= 4	Count and Add Only Aces						
Fives	= 5	Count and Add Only Aces						
Sixes	= 6	Count and Add Only Aces						
TOTAL SCORE		→						
BONUS	If total score is 63 or over	SCORE 35						
TOTAL	Of upper Section	→						

LOWER SECTION

			GAME #1	GAME #2	GAME #3	GAME #4	GAME #5	GAME #6
3 of a kind		Add Total Of All Dice						
4 of a kind		Add Total Of All Dice						
Full House		SCORE 25						
Sm. Straight	Sequence of 4	SCORE 30						
Lg. Straight	Sequence of 5	SCORE 40						
YAHTZEE	of 5 a kind	SCORE 50						
Chance		Score Total Of All 5 Dice						
YAHTZEE BONUS		FOR EACH BONUS						
		SCORE 100 PER						
TOTAL	Of Lower Section	→						
TOTAL	Of Upper Section	→						
GRAND TOTAL		→						

Yahtzee Score Sheet

UPPER SECTION		HOW TO SCORE	GAME #1	GAME #2	GAME #3	GAME #4	GAME #5	GAME #6
Aces	• = 1	Count and Add Only Aces						
Twos	= 2	Count and Add Only Aces						
Threes	= 3	Count and Add Only Aces						
Fours	= 4	Count and Add Only Aces						
Fives	= 5	Count and Add Only Aces						
Sixes	= 6	Count and Add Only Aces						
TOTAL SCORE		→						
BONUS	If total score is 63 or over	SCORE 35						
TOTAL	Of upper Section	→						

LOWER SECTION

			GAME #1	GAME #2	GAME #3	GAME #4	GAME #5	GAME #6
3 of a kind		Add Total Of All Dice						
4 of a kind		Add Total Of All Dice						
Full House		SCORE 25						
Sm. Straight	Sequence of 4	SCORE 30						
Lg. Straight	Sequence of 5	SCORE 40						
YAHTZEE	of 5 a kind	SCORE 50						
Chance		Score Total Of All 5 Dice						
YAHTZEE BONUS		FOR EACH BONUS						
		SCORE 100 PER						
TOTAL	Of Lower Section	→						
TOTAL	Of Upper Section	→						
GRAND TOTAL		→						

Yahtzee Score Sheet

UPPER SECTION		HOW TO SCORE	GAME #1	GAME #2	GAME #3	GAME #4	GAME #5	GAME #6
Aces	• = 1	Count and Add Only Aces						
Twos	: = 2	Count and Add Only Aces						
Threes	⋰ = 3	Count and Add Only Aces						
Fours	:: = 4	Count and Add Only Aces						
Fives	:·: = 5	Count and Add Only Aces						
Sixes	::: = 6	Count and Add Only Aces						
TOTAL SCORE		→						
BONUS	If total score is 63 or over	SCORE 35						
TOTAL	Of upper Section	→						

LOWER SECTION

		HOW TO SCORE	GAME #1	GAME #2	GAME #3	GAME #4	GAME #5	GAME #6
3 of a kind		Add Total Of All Dice						
4 of a kind		Add Total Of All Dice						
Full House		SCORE 25						
Sm. Straight	Sequence of 4	SCORE 30						
Lg. Straight	Sequence of 5	SCORE 40						
YAHTZEE	of 5 a kind	SCORE 50						
Chance		Score Total Of All 5 Dice						
YAHTZEE BONUS		FOR EACH BONUS						
		SCORE 100 PER						
TOTAL	Of Lower Section	→						
TOTAL	Of Upper Section	→						
GRAND TOTAL		→						

Yahtzee Score Sheet

UPPER SECTION		HOW TO SCORE	GAME #1	GAME #2	GAME #3	GAME #4	GAME #5	GAME #6
Aces	• = 1	Count and Add Only Aces						
Twos	• • = 2	Count and Add Only Aces						
Threes	• • • = 3	Count and Add Only Aces						
Fours	• • • • = 4	Count and Add Only Aces						
Fives	• • • • • = 5	Count and Add Only Aces						
Sixes	• • • • • • = 6	Count and Add Only Aces						
TOTAL SCORE		→						
BONUS	If total score is 63 or over	SCORE 35						
TOTAL	Of upper Section	→						

LOWER SECTION

		HOW TO SCORE	GAME #1	GAME #2	GAME #3	GAME #4	GAME #5	GAME #6
3 of a kind		Add Total Of All Dice						
4 of a kind		Add Total Of All Dice						
Full House		SCORE 25						
Sm. Straight	Sequence of 4	SCORE 30						
Lg. Straight	Sequence of 5	SCORE 40						
YAHTZEE	of 5 a kind	SCORE 50						
Chance		Score Total Of All 5 Dice						
YAHTZEE BONUS		FOR EACH BONUS						
		SCORE 100 PER						
TOTAL	Of Lower Section	→						
TOTAL	Of Upper Section	→						
GRAND TOTAL		→						

Yahtzee Score Sheet

UPPER SECTION		HOW TO SCORE	GAME #1	GAME #2	GAME #3	GAME #4	GAME #5	GAME #6
Aces	• = 1	Count and Add Only Aces						
Twos	= 2	Count and Add Only Aces						
Threes	= 3	Count and Add Only Aces						
Fours	= 4	Count and Add Only Aces						
Fives	= 5	Count and Add Only Aces						
Sixes	= 6	Count and Add Only Aces						
TOTAL SCORE		→						
BONUS	If total score is 63 or over	SCORE 35						
TOTAL	Of upper Section	→						

LOWER SECTION

			GAME #1	GAME #2	GAME #3	GAME #4	GAME #5	GAME #6
3 of a kind		Add Total Of All Dice						
4 of a kind		Add Total Of All Dice						
Full House		SCORE 25						
Sm. Straight	Sequence of 4	SCORE 30						
Lg. Straight	Sequence of 5	SCORE 40						
YAHTZEE	of 5 a kind	SCORE 50						
Chance		Score Total Of All 5 Dice						
YAHTZEE BONUS		FOR EACH BONUS						
		SCORE 100 PER						
TOTAL	Of Lower Section	→						
TOTAL	Of Upper Section	→						
GRAND TOTAL		→						

Yahtzee Score Sheet

UPPER SECTION		HOW TO SCORE	GAME #1	GAME #2	GAME #3	GAME #4	GAME #5	GAME #6
Aces	= 1	Count and Add Only Aces						
Twos	= 2	Count and Add Only Aces						
Threes	= 3	Count and Add Only Aces						
Fours	= 4	Count and Add Only Aces						
Fives	= 5	Count and Add Only Aces						
Sixes	= 6	Count and Add Only Aces						
TOTAL SCORE		→						
BONUS If total score is 63 or over		SCORE 35						
TOTAL Of upper Section		→						

LOWER SECTION

		HOW TO SCORE	GAME #1	GAME #2	GAME #3	GAME #4	GAME #5	GAME #6
3 of a kind		Add Total Of All Dice						
4 of a kind		Add Total Of All Dice						
Full House		SCORE 25						
Sm. Straight	Sequence of 4	SCORE 30						
Lg. Straight	Sequence of 5	SCORE 40						
YAHTZEE	of 5 a kind	SCORE 50						
Chance		Score Total Of All 5 Dice						
YAHTZEE BONUS		FOR EACH BONUS						
		SCORE 100 PER						
TOTAL Of Lower Section		→						
TOTAL Of Upper Section		→						
GRAND TOTAL		→						

Yahtzee Score Sheet

UPPER SECTION		HOW TO SCORE	GAME #1	GAME #2	GAME #3	GAME #4	GAME #5	GAME #6
Aces	• = 1	Count and Add Only Aces						
Twos	= 2	Count and Add Only Aces						
Threes	= 3	Count and Add Only Aces						
Fours	= 4	Count and Add Only Aces						
Fives	= 5	Count and Add Only Aces						
Sixes	= 6	Count and Add Only Aces						
TOTAL SCORE		⟶						
BONUS — If total score is 63 or over		SCORE 35						
TOTAL — Of upper Section		⟶						

LOWER SECTION

	HOW TO SCORE	GAME #1	GAME #2	GAME #3	GAME #4	GAME #5	GAME #6
3 of a kind	Add Total Of All Dice						
4 of a kind	Add Total Of All Dice						
Full House	SCORE 25						
Sm. Straight — Sequence of 4	SCORE 30						
Lg. Straight — Sequence of 5	SCORE 40						
YAHTZEE — of 5 a kind	SCORE 50						
Chance	Score Total Of All 5 Dice						
YAHTZEE BONUS	FOR EACH BONUS						
	SCORE 100 PER						
TOTAL — Of Lower Section	⟶						
TOTAL — Of Upper Section	⟶						
GRAND TOTAL	⟶						

Yahtzee Score Sheet

UPPER SECTION		HOW TO SCORE	GAME #1	GAME #2	GAME #3	GAME #4	GAME #5	GAME #6
Aces	• = 1	Count and Add Only Aces						
Twos	•• = 2	Count and Add Only Aces						
Threes	••• = 3	Count and Add Only Aces						
Fours	•••• = 4	Count and Add Only Aces						
Fives	••••• = 5	Count and Add Only Aces						
Sixes	•••••• = 6	Count and Add Only Aces						
TOTAL SCORE		→						
BONUS	If total score is 63 or over	SCORE 35						
TOTAL	Of upper Section	→						

LOWER SECTION

LOWER SECTION		HOW TO SCORE	GAME #1	GAME #2	GAME #3	GAME #4	GAME #5	GAME #6
3 of a kind		Add Total Of All Dice						
4 of a kind		Add Total Of All Dice						
Full House		SCORE 25						
Sm. Straight	Sequence of 4	SCORE 30						
Lg. Straight	Sequence of 5	SCORE 40						
YAHTZEE	of 5 a kind	SCORE 50						
Chance		Score Total Of All 5 Dice						
YAHTZEE BONUS		FOR EACH BONUS						
		SCORE 100 PER						
TOTAL	Of Lower Section	→						
TOTAL	Of Upper Section	→						
GRAND TOTAL		→						

Yahtzee Score Sheet

UPPER SECTION		HOW TO SCORE	GAME #1	GAME #2	GAME #3	GAME #4	GAME #5	GAME #6
Aces	= 1	Count and Add Only Aces						
Twos	= 2	Count and Add Only Aces						
Threes	= 3	Count and Add Only Aces						
Fours	= 4	Count and Add Only Aces						
Fives	= 5	Count and Add Only Aces						
Sixes	= 6	Count and Add Only Aces						
TOTAL SCORE		→						
BONUS	If total score is 63 or over	SCORE 35						
TOTAL	Of upper Section	→						

LOWER SECTION

		HOW TO SCORE	GAME #1	GAME #2	GAME #3	GAME #4	GAME #5	GAME #6
3 of a kind		Add Total Of All Dice						
4 of a kind		Add Total Of All Dice						
Full House		SCORE 25						
Sm. Straight	Sequence of 4	SCORE 30						
Lg. Straight	Sequence of 5	SCORE 40						
YAHTZEE	of 5 a kind	SCORE 50						
Chance		Score Total Of All 5 Dice						
YAHTZEE BONUS		FOR EACH BONUS						
		SCORE 100 PER						
TOTAL	Of Lower Section	→						
TOTAL	Of Upper Section	→						
GRAND TOTAL		→						

Yahtzee Score Sheet

UPPER SECTION			HOW TO SCORE	GAME #1	GAME #2	GAME #3	GAME #4	GAME #5	GAME #6
Aces	•	= 1	Count and Add Only Aces						
Twos		= 2	Count and Add Only Aces						
Threes		= 3	Count and Add Only Aces						
Fours		= 4	Count and Add Only Aces						
Fives		= 5	Count and Add Only Aces						
Sixes		= 6	Count and Add Only Aces						
TOTAL SCORE		⟶							
BONUS	If total score is 63 or over		SCORE 35						
TOTAL	Of upper Section	⟶							

LOWER SECTION

				GAME #1	GAME #2	GAME #3	GAME #4	GAME #5	GAME #6
3 of a kind		Add Total Of All Dice							
4 of a kind		Add Total Of All Dice							
Full House		SCORE 25							
Sm. Straight	Sequence of 4	SCORE 30							
Lg. Straight	Sequence of 5	SCORE 40							
YAHTZEE	of 5 a kind	SCORE 50							
Chance		Score Total Of All 5 Dice							
YAHTZEE BONUS		FOR EACH BONUS							
		SCORE 100 PER							
TOTAL	Of Lower Section	⟶							
TOTAL	Of Upper Section	⟶							
GRAND TOTAL		⟶							

Yahtzee Score Sheet

UPPER SECTION		HOW TO SCORE	GAME #1	GAME #2	GAME #3	GAME #4	GAME #5	GAME #6
Aces	• = 1	Count and Add Only Aces						
Twos	•• = 2	Count and Add Only Aces						
Threes	••• = 3	Count and Add Only Aces						
Fours	•••• = 4	Count and Add Only Aces						
Fives	••••• = 5	Count and Add Only Aces						
Sixes	•••••• = 6	Count and Add Only Aces						
TOTAL SCORE		→						
BONUS	If total score is 63 or over	SCORE 35						
TOTAL	Of upper Section	→						

LOWER SECTION

		HOW TO SCORE	GAME #1	GAME #2	GAME #3	GAME #4	GAME #5	GAME #6
3 of a kind		Add Total Of All Dice						
4 of a kind		Add Total Of All Dice						
Full House		SCORE 25						
Sm. Straight	Sequence of 4	SCORE 30						
Lg. Straight	Sequence of 5	SCORE 40						
YAHTZEE	of 5 a kind	SCORE 50						
Chance		Score Total Of All 5 Dice						
YAHTZEE BONUS		FOR EACH BONUS						
		SCORE 100 PER						
TOTAL	Of Lower Section	→						
TOTAL	Of Upper Section	→						
GRAND TOTAL		→						

Yahtzee Score Sheet

UPPER SECTION	HOW TO SCORE	GAME #1	GAME #2	GAME #3	GAME #4	GAME #5	GAME #6
Aces • = 1	Count and Add Only Aces						
Twos • = 2	Count and Add Only Aces						
Threes • = 3	Count and Add Only Aces						
Fours • = 4	Count and Add Only Aces						
Fives • = 5	Count and Add Only Aces						
Sixes • = 6	Count and Add Only Aces						
TOTAL SCORE	→						
BONUS If total score is 63 or over	SCORE 35						
TOTAL Of upper Section	→						

LOWER SECTION

	HOW TO SCORE	GAME #1	GAME #2	GAME #3	GAME #4	GAME #5	GAME #6
3 of a kind	Add Total Of All Dice						
4 of a kind	Add Total Of All Dice						
Full House	SCORE 25						
Sm. Straight Sequence of 4	SCORE 30						
Lg. Straight Sequence of 5	SCORE 40						
YAHTZEE of 5 a kind	SCORE 50						
Chance	Score Total Of All 5 Dice						
YAHTZEE BONUS	FOR EACH BONUS						
	SCORE 100 PER						
TOTAL Of Lower Section	→						
TOTAL Of Upper Section	→						
GRAND TOTAL	→						

Yahtzee Score Sheet

UPPER SECTION		HOW TO SCORE	GAME #1	GAME #2	GAME #3	GAME #4	GAME #5	GAME #6
Aces	= 1	Count and Add Only Aces						
Twos	= 2	Count and Add Only Aces						
Threes	= 3	Count and Add Only Aces						
Fours	= 4	Count and Add Only Aces						
Fives	= 5	Count and Add Only Aces						
Sixes	= 6	Count and Add Only Aces						
TOTAL SCORE		→						
BONUS — If total score is 63 or over		SCORE 35						
TOTAL — Of upper Section		→						

LOWER SECTION

	HOW TO SCORE	GAME #1	GAME #2	GAME #3	GAME #4	GAME #5	GAME #6
3 of a kind	Add Total Of All Dice						
4 of a kind	Add Total Of All Dice						
Full House	SCORE 25						
Sm. Straight — Sequence of 4	SCORE 30						
Lg. Straight — Sequence of 5	SCORE 40						
YAHTZEE — of 5 a kind	SCORE 50						
Chance	Score Total Of All 5 Dice						
YAHTZEE BONUS	FOR EACH BONUS						
	SCORE 100 PER						
TOTAL — Of Lower Section	→						
TOTAL — Of Upper Section	→						
GRAND TOTAL	→						

Yahtzee Score Sheet

UPPER SECTION		HOW TO SCORE	GAME #1	GAME #2	GAME #3	GAME #4	GAME #5	GAME #6
Aces	= 1	Count and Add Only Aces						
Twos	= 2	Count and Add Only Aces						
Threes	= 3	Count and Add Only Aces						
Fours	= 4	Count and Add Only Aces						
Fives	= 5	Count and Add Only Aces						
Sixes	= 6	Count and Add Only Aces						
TOTAL SCORE		→						
BONUS	If total score is 63 or over	SCORE 35						
TOTAL	Of upper Section	→						

LOWER SECTION

			GAME #1	GAME #2	GAME #3	GAME #4	GAME #5	GAME #6
3 of a kind		Add Total Of All Dice						
4 of a kind		Add Total Of All Dice						
Full House		SCORE 25						
Sm. Straight	Sequence of 4	SCORE 30						
Lg. Straight	Sequence of 5	SCORE 40						
YAHTZEE	of 5 a kind	SCORE 50						
Chance		Score Total Of All 5 Dice						
YAHTZEE BONUS		FOR EACH BONUS						
		SCORE 100 PER						
TOTAL	Of Lower Section	→						
TOTAL	Of Upper Section	→						
GRAND TOTAL		→						

Yahtzee Score Sheet

UPPER SECTION		HOW TO SCORE	GAME #1	GAME #2	GAME #3	GAME #4	GAME #5	GAME #6
Aces	= 1	Count and Add Only Aces						
Twos	= 2	Count and Add Only Aces						
Threes	= 3	Count and Add Only Aces						
Fours	= 4	Count and Add Only Aces						
Fives	= 5	Count and Add Only Aces						
Sixes	= 6	Count and Add Only Aces						
TOTAL SCORE		→						
BONUS	If total score is 63 or over	SCORE 35						
TOTAL	Of upper Section	→						

LOWER SECTION

			GAME #1	GAME #2	GAME #3	GAME #4	GAME #5	GAME #6
3 of a kind		Add Total Of All Dice						
4 of a kind		Add Total Of All Dice						
Full House		SCORE 25						
Sm. Straight	Sequence of 4	SCORE 30						
Lg. Straight	Sequence of 5	SCORE 40						
YAHTZEE	of 5 a kind	SCORE 50						
Chance		Score Total Of All 5 Dice						
YAHTZEE BONUS		FOR EACH BONUS						
		SCORE 100 PER						
TOTAL	Of Lower Section	→						
TOTAL	Of Upper Section	→						
GRAND TOTAL		→						

Yahtzee Score Sheet

UPPER SECTION		HOW TO SCORE	GAME #1	GAME #2	GAME #3	GAME #4	GAME #5	GAME #6
Aces	= 1	Count and Add Only Aces						
Twos	= 2	Count and Add Only Aces						
Threes	= 3	Count and Add Only Aces						
Fours	= 4	Count and Add Only Aces						
Fives	= 5	Count and Add Only Aces						
Sixes	= 6	Count and Add Only Aces						
TOTAL SCORE		→						
BONUS — If total score is 63 or over		SCORE 35						
TOTAL — Of upper Section		→						

LOWER SECTION

	HOW TO SCORE	GAME #1	GAME #2	GAME #3	GAME #4	GAME #5	GAME #6
3 of a kind	Add Total Of All Dice						
4 of a kind	Add Total Of All Dice						
Full House	SCORE 25						
Sm. Straight — Sequence of 4	SCORE 30						
Lg. Straight — Sequence of 5	SCORE 40						
YAHTZEE — of 5 a kind	SCORE 50						
Chance	Score Total Of All 5 Dice						
YAHTZEE BONUS	FOR EACH BONUS						
YAHTZEE BONUS	SCORE 100 PER						
TOTAL — Of Lower Section	→						
TOTAL — Of Upper Section	→						
GRAND TOTAL	→						

Yahtzee Score Sheet

UPPER SECTION		HOW TO SCORE	GAME #1	GAME #2	GAME #3	GAME #4	GAME #5	GAME #6
Aces	= 1	Count and Add Only Aces						
Twos	= 2	Count and Add Only Aces						
Threes	= 3	Count and Add Only Aces						
Fours	= 4	Count and Add Only Aces						
Fives	= 5	Count and Add Only Aces						
Sixes	= 6	Count and Add Only Aces						
TOTAL SCORE		→						
BONUS If total score is 63 or over		SCORE 35						
TOTAL Of upper Section		→						

LOWER SECTION

	HOW TO SCORE	GAME #1	GAME #2	GAME #3	GAME #4	GAME #5	GAME #6
3 of a kind	Add Total Of All Dice						
4 of a kind	Add Total Of All Dice						
Full House	SCORE 25						
Sm. Straight Sequence of 4	SCORE 30						
Lg. Straight Sequence of 5	SCORE 40						
YAHTZEE of 5 a kind	SCORE 50						
Chance	Score Total Of All 5 Dice						
YAHTZEE BONUS	FOR EACH BONUS						
	SCORE 100 PER						
TOTAL Of Lower Section	→						
TOTAL Of Upper Section	→						
GRAND TOTAL	→						

Yahtzee Score Sheet

UPPER SECTION		HOW TO SCORE	GAME #1	GAME #2	GAME #3	GAME #4	GAME #5	GAME #6
Aces	= 1	Count and Add Only Aces						
Twos	= 2	Count and Add Only Aces						
Threes	= 3	Count and Add Only Aces						
Fours	= 4	Count and Add Only Aces						
Fives	= 5	Count and Add Only Aces						
Sixes	= 6	Count and Add Only Aces						
TOTAL SCORE		→						
BONUS	If total score is 63 or over	SCORE 35						
TOTAL	Of upper Section	→						

LOWER SECTION

			GAME #1	GAME #2	GAME #3	GAME #4	GAME #5	GAME #6
3 of a kind		Add Total Of All Dice						
4 of a kind		Add Total Of All Dice						
Full House		SCORE 25						
Sm. Straight	Sequence of 4	SCORE 30						
Lg. Straight	Sequence of 5	SCORE 40						
YAHTZEE	of 5 a kind	SCORE 50						
Chance		Score Total Of All 5 Dice						
YAHTZEE BONUS		FOR EACH BONUS						
		SCORE 100 PER						
TOTAL	Of Lower Section	→						
TOTAL	Of Upper Section	→						
GRAND TOTAL		→						

Yahtzee Score Sheet

UPPER SECTION		HOW TO SCORE	GAME #1	GAME #2	GAME #3	GAME #4	GAME #5	GAME #6
Aces	• = 1	Count and Add Only Aces						
Twos	•• = 2	Count and Add Only Aces						
Threes	••• = 3	Count and Add Only Aces						
Fours	•••• = 4	Count and Add Only Aces						
Fives	••••• = 5	Count and Add Only Aces						
Sixes	•••••• = 6	Count and Add Only Aces						
TOTAL SCORE		→						
BONUS If total score is 63 or over		SCORE 35						
TOTAL Of upper Section		→						

LOWER SECTION

	HOW TO SCORE	GAME #1	GAME #2	GAME #3	GAME #4	GAME #5	GAME #6
3 of a kind	Add Total Of All Dice						
4 of a kind	Add Total Of All Dice						
Full House	SCORE 25						
Sm. Straight Sequence of 4	SCORE 30						
Lg. Straight Sequence of 5	SCORE 40						
YAHTZEE of 5 a kind	SCORE 50						
Chance	Score Total Of All 5 Dice						
YAHTZEE BONUS	FOR EACH BONUS						
	SCORE 100 PER						
TOTAL Of Lower Section	→						
TOTAL Of Upper Section	→						
GRAND TOTAL	→						